Alex Matthews

Elder Abuse:

The New Normal?

*How to prevent
elder abuse at care homes
A guide for clients and their relatives*

Alex Matthews

Elder abuse: The new normal?
How to prevent elder abuse at care homes. A guide for clients and their relatives.

Published by KDP
ISBN: 9781790290758
Available on Kindle e-book and Amazon paperback
Cover design by Alex Matthews
Author's blog - http://isladeoro.blogspot.co.uk/
All content copyright of Alex Matthews 2016/2018. All rights are reserved.

First published by Pavilion Publishing and Media Ltd in 2016 under the title *She'll be Alright: a story-based approach to exploring issues of hidden neglect in care homes. A training and self-study guide with a focus on dementia care.* ISBN: 978-1-911028-38-3. This new 2019 version is published with permission obtained from Pavilion Publishing and Media Ltd in 2018.

Contents

Introduction and Foreword	1
Brutal Care	5
This Is Not Happening	13
Tom's Hand	21
Elsie's Men	27
Pyjama Party	33
Big Ron's Bed	39
The Party of Endearment	47
10 Minutes	55
Hitler Is Alive	61
Set 4	69
Smeared Pages	81
True Love	89
Epilogue	91
Conclusion	95
Appendix 1 – Fundamental Care Standards	97
Appendix 2 – Code of Conduct for Healthcare Support Workers and Adult Social Care Workers in England	111
Author's bibliography	123

Alex Matthews

Although the advice in this book is intended for the UK, it is also relevant in countries such as Australia, New Zealand, Canada and the US, where social care challenges are very similar.

Acknowledgements

I would like to thank my main proof readers Susie, Francis and my mother for their suggestions. Also, many thanks to the healthcare professionals who read the first manuscript and offered opinion and support.

Foreword by the author

The stories presented here focus on hidden neglect in care homes – neglect that goes unnoticed because it is not visible. The author believes that exposing where care goes wrong gives the reader the chance to work out why, and then explore how the problems could be avoided. This analytical process may be much more useful in practice than giving examples of perfect care. But, of course, the writer has also worked with excellent carers and nurses who are worthy of mention and praise. I do not want the reader to get the impression that all carers 'go rogue'. However, I hope that these powerful stories will make a positive contribution to enhancing management and care practice across all care settings.

Alex Matthews

Introduction

The first version of this book was published by Pavilion Publishing and Media Ltd in 2016 as a training guide for carers and managers under the title *She'll be Alright: a story-based approach to exploring issues of hidden neglect in care homes. A training and self-study guide with a focus on dementia care*. The book features twelve stories of neglect and abuse witnessed by the author while he was working at nursing homes four years ago. It is now the year 2019 and the problems of abuse and neglect in British care homes haven't improved at all since the first version of this book was published. These twelve stories of neglect and abuse presented here are, therefore, as current today as they were three years ago. If the first version is a training guide, this new version focuses more on explaining to the wider public why and how abuse happens, as well as on how to prevent it.

News about neglect and abuse exposed by the media today mirror exactly the stories in this book; such is the extent and standardisation of abuse. A March 21, 2018 study by University College London (UCL) asked more than 1,500 carers at 92 homes across the UK if they had witnessed, or taken part in, troubling behaviour in the past three months. At least some abuse or neglect was identified in 91 out of the 92 care homes, and by more than half of respondents. What this means is that 99 percent of care homes in the UK are at risk of staging abuse at some point. Again, the behaviours and attitudes in the UCL research mirror exactly the neglect and abuse in the twelve stories that follow: carers not having enough time to provide good personal care, or residents having to wait long hours for a pad change. The fact that this type of malpractice is so widespread means that those who are contemplating moving into a care home can expect neglect and abuse almost by default.

Indeed, as soon as you enter the care home and your relatives have left, the neglect will start. Why do we know this? Because under current legislation, care homes are not required to have a minimum number of carers per resident, so only two carers for every twelve to fifteen residents is the staffing ratio you will find across all care homes. This ratio is too low because most complex care requires two carers, which means that if you need care urgently, you will have to wait. But, of course, someone else will also have been waiting for care before you, so a backlog of residents' care is formed. This means that, in order to provide care for everyone, carers need to rush and cut corners, which leads to poor personal hygiene, malnutrition, dehydration, and high levels of infection. Therefore, one could describe the current crisis in social care as *neglect by State* until a ratio of at least three carers for every twelve residents is established and enforced.

©Alex Matthews 2018

In contrast, the *State of Care 2017/2018* report published by the Care Quality Commission rates 79 per cent of social care services as good, 3 percent are rated as outstanding, only 17 percent as requiring improvement, and a mere 1 per cent are inadequate. When, as everyone knows, the truth is that the whole of the social care system is inadequate. Even the very CQC contradict themselves when, in the same email newsletter with the *State of Care 2017/2018* report, they declare a virtual state of emergency:

'Two years ago we warned social care was 'approaching a tipping point' - as unmet needs continue to rise, this tipping point has already been reached for some people who are not getting the care they need.' - Ian Trenholm, Chief Executive CQC

With 82 per cent of services rated as good or outstanding, how can we be approaching a tipping point? We'll leave the CQC to ponder about that one. In the meantime, people in care homes will be abused by the thousands. People receiving care in their own homes will spend the whole day alone, sitting in front of the TV, in a wet pad, unable to move or even change channels, except for their three short care visits a day, when they will get their medication and be left with a meal and a cup of tea in front of them.

The fact is, social care in the UK reached that tipping point a long time ago so, when you enter the care system you won't only be hit by extortionate rates, you are going to face abuse right from the beginning. This book will give you an invaluable insight into the care home world and on how to prevent becoming the victim of abuse.

The power of storytelling

Elder abuse: The new normal? is a series of short episodes showing neglect in an English nursing home. These are the stories of people who can no longer speak for themselves and invite the reader to access the world of care as it unfolds behind closed doors. The characters' real names have been changed and the events have been slightly altered in order to create works of fiction, but the stories presented here are true in essence.

Exploring neglect through stories gives the reader a chance to reflect on its causes and discover its roots in care management, human resources, staffing levels, and training of staff, and to realise how these underlying problems can negatively affect service users.

The author is a teacher turned carer who was puzzled by the contradictions and neglect he encountered within luxury care settings. The writer thinks that the social care system needs a complete overhaul in order to deliver services that are adequate, compassionate and efficient. A new model of social care needs to replace the current one, but the political and social will is not there at all. No positive change has come forward from the industry, the political establishment, or society at large in the long years that the social care system has been in deep crisis. The terms *social care crisis, social care time-bomb,* and *social care tipping point,* are so common that they have become a part of the care landscape in a new paradigm where abuse is seen as business as usual. Therefore, the idea that someone in the system is going to come up with a solution seems increasingly unlikely. It is up to individuals and families to get together and fight for themselves, independently. This book will show you, step by step, how to apply current legislation in order to uncover abuse and how to disclose it correctly. It is this writer's experience that care home residents whose relatives take an active part in their care get much better quality care than the rest. So read on and learn how to take direct action in order to stop abuse before it can even happen.

How to use this book

Each case of malpractice in the stories has a footnote pointing to the relevant piece of legislation being violated, in this case, the *Fundamental Care Standards.* Also the *Code of Conduct for Healthcare Support Workers and Adult Social Care Workers in England* is made reference to in the footnotes. This will allow the reader to understand what constitutes neglect and abuse and, therefore, learn how to articulate complaints within the right legislative framework.

There is also a reflection section after every chapter with a *point of advice* that explains what action could be taken in order to remedy or prevent the malpractice. This is followed by another section with positive advice for care home managers on how to improve the service provided to you.

Going through the stories, the legislation, and the reflection sections, will allow you to gain a crucial insight into some of the challenges facing care homes, as well as to get the knowledge you need in order to protect yourself or a family member who is a user of the care system.

A note on the reflection sections

The answers to the questions that follow each case study are mainly based on the European Charter of Human Rights, the Fundamental Care Standards, and the Code of Conduct for Healthcare Support Workers and Adult Social Care Workers in England. While a lot of thought and care has gone into preparing these sample answers, please be aware that they are neither intended to be comprehensive nor the last word on social care. Additional answers should come up as you reflect and discuss the issues in the case studies.

As regards the questions themselves, they are by no means an exhaustive list. The case studies presented in *Elder Abuse: The new normal?* should pose many more questions that will help you delve into the topic of safeguarding against neglect and abuse.

Brutal Care

Harry hasn't spoken for quite a long time. He can't even answer yes or no. A faint murmur is all he is capable of. His eyes don't usually focus on anything in particular. And he is as stiff as a plank.

The tall carer in the polo shirt is looking at the rota for this morning. He and his partner have twelve residents on their list[1]. Gill is independent, we'll just need to keep an eye on her. Richard only needs a little help with his morning wash. That still leaves ten. Ten residents, and only two hours before breakfast. This is not going to be nice at all.

Donna is not happy this morning. Not only does she have to get ten residents up, washed and dressed in less than two hours, but she has been paired up with an amateur, so this shift is going to be extra hard for her.

Loud rock music plays in Harry's room. A ray of morning light falls on his bedside table. An old mobile phone. A wrist watch. Reading glasses. His eyes are closed. There is a knock at the door.

'Has the radio been on all night long?'

'That's what the wife wants.'

'How awful! Good morning, Harry.'

Harry's bed is raised a bit higher, so the work is easier for the carers. Since the tangles and plaques invaded, his memory has been a bit of a mess, but this pulling and pushing is quite familiar to him. He can feel something like robot pincers grab his arms while bulldozer hands push him one way and then the other. His night time clothes are stripped off by the same heavy machinery. *Rip* goes his pyjama top[2].

---

[1] **Care Standards**: 18. *Staffing.* (1) Sufficient numbers of suitably qualified, competent, skilled and experienced persons must be deployed in order to meet the requirements of this Part.

[2] **Care Standards**: 13. *Safeguarding service users from abuse and improper treatment.*
(1) Service users must be protected from abuse and improper treatment in accordance with this regulation. (2) Systems and processes must be established and operated effectively to prevent abuse of service users. (3) Systems and processes must be established and operated effectively to investigate, immediately upon becoming aware of, any allegation or evidence of such abuse. (4) Care or treatment for service users must not be provided in a way that— (a) includes discrimination against a service user on grounds of any protected characteristic (as defined in section 4 of the Equality Act 2010) of the service user, (b) includes acts

©Alex Matthews 2018

'Oh, dear!'

'It's the relatives. They don't think, do they? They buy clothes that don't fit.'

One of the carers is not too convinced that this can be called caring for somebody. But he is new on the job and doesn't have the backbone to tell the other carer to stop the harsh handling. The company policies say that we must obtain consent before we attempt any action. That we must watch out for signs of consent when the person can't speak. We know that we have to communicate with the client, that we must inform them before any care is performed. But then we would spend two hours just on Harry. And everyone else would have to have breakfast in bed in an uncomfortable wet pad. Perhaps Donna is doing the right thing, given the circumstances.

A seaman, he had been. Although he has the looks and poise of a Franciscan monk now, with that beard and the lost expression of someone entranced in deep meditation. He had been to Brazil, to pre-Castro Cuba, Lebanon, China. If he could speak he could tell stories about starry nights in Middle Eastern oases, of wild New York stop overs, and of friendly people he met in Pacific islands. But, except for his wife's once-a-week visit, no one comes to see him.

Harry is now naked on his bed. He gets a fast wash. But at least he gets a wash. Donna can remember days when only a pad change was possible for all residents. So what are you complaining about? You don't know what it's like, so shut up! I do care, you know.

There is more shoving and rolling. This time, to get Harry dressed. Somebody is going through the motions. Confused. Is this really happening? There is a violent jerk, and *rip* goes the shirt. There is no need for words.

---

intended to control or restrain a service user that are not necessary to prevent, or not a proportionate response to, a risk of harm posed to the service user or another individual if the service user was not subject to control or restraint, (c) is degrading for the service user, or (d) significantly disregards the needs of the service user for care or treatment. (5) A service user must not be deprived of their liberty for the purpose of receiving care or treatment without lawful authority. (6) For the purposes of this regulation— "abuse" means— (a) any behaviour towards a service user that is an offence under the Sexual Offences Act 2003(a), (b) ill-treatment (whether of a physical or psychological nature) of a service user, (c) theft, misuse or misappropriation of money or property belonging to a service user, or (d) neglect of a service user. (7) For the purposes of this regulation, a person controls or restrains a service user if that person— (a) uses, or threatens to use, force to secure the doing of an act which the service user resists, or (b) restricts the service user's liberty of movement, whether or not the service user resists, including by use of physical, mechanical or chemical means.

©Alex Matthews 2018

'Look, I know what you are thinking, but if we take too long being nice to Harry, we have nine other people swimming in their own urine. And they too suffer. We need to get to them before breakfast. That's what I care about. Because I do care. Even if you think I don't.' [3]

'Point taken.'

Now that she's made herself clear, Donna does have a licence to kill. And the pulling becomes as hard as the body is stiff. Harry needs to sit up on the edge of the bed now, so he can be helped into his wheelchair with a stand aid. But the idiot in the polo shirt is not cooperating in spite of the lecture. Now, with the power of a crow bar, she unlocks the joints. You will sit up. A wrench is felt as Donna hauls hard at the arms and shoulders.[4]

Perhaps Harry was never seasick. Perhaps he wasn't afraid of sea storms. Maybe the man was bigger than the waves. Because now that big man inside has been awakened. His fierce eyes fixed on the carers' eyes.

'What do you think you are doing! Knock it off!'

---

[3] **Care Standards**: *19. Fit and proper persons employed.* (1) Persons employed for the purposes of carrying on a regulated activity must— (a) be of good character.

[4] **Code of Conduct 2:** *Promote and uphold the privacy, dignity, rights, health and wellbeing of people who use health and care services and their carers at all times.* As a Healthcare Support Worker or Adult Social Care Worker in England you must:
1. always act in the best interests of people who use health and care services.
2. always treat people with respect and compassion.
3. put the needs, goals and aspirations of people who use health and care services first, helping them to be in control and to choose the healthcare, care and support they receive.
4. promote people's independence and ability to self-care, assisting those who use health and care services to exercise their rights and make informed choices.
5. always gain valid consent before providing healthcare, care and support. You must also respect a person's right to refuse to receive healthcare, care and support if they are capable of doing so.
6. always maintain the privacy and dignity of people who use health and care services, their carers and others.
7. be alert to any changes that could affect a person's needs or progress and report your observations in line with your employer's agreed ways of working.
8. always make sure that your actions or omissions do not harm an individual's health or wellbeing. You must never abuse, neglect, harm or exploit those who use health and care services, their carers or your colleagues.
9. challenge and report dangerous, abusive, discriminatory or exploitative behaviour or practice.
10. always take comments and complaints seriously, respond to them in line with agreed ways of working and inform a senior member of staff.

©Alex Matthews 2018

And no sooner do these words leave his lips than he is back sailing the dark seas of neurone malfunction.

Donna doesn't seem bemused by the fact that Harry has actually spoken. Too busy and angry. Embarrassed to be caught in the act like this, maybe. But the other carer is dumbfounded. Harry is actually capable of perfect intelligible speech. He is still there.

The master of the waves has been subdued into submission and is now hooked up to a crane and going up. Arms up, the force of the machine snaps and straightens the locked joints. His leg muscles hardly bearing his own weight, he hangs like a modern Jesus. His trousers are done up. His wheelchair readied for the landing. But this storm of care is proving too much for the old sailor and a loud growling splatter is heard.

'Oh, no. You must be joking!'

'I'll go get sanitiser and everything else.'

'No. The resident's safety comes first. Let's push him into the bathroom and shower him.'

'But this stuff is going to go everywhere.'

'Never mind that now. We'll wash him first.'

Harry had seen the world. In his picture album you could see him in foreign places, even visiting the holy land of Jerusalem at a time when few pilgrims dared make that journey. Could he have guessed then that he would end up crucified in a cold bathroom? Looking at Harry's photo album, pictures of a modern Christ is what you see in the last page. His brain still sailing seas unknown, though; a wild spark still able to stand up to storms.

Main points of advice

Visiting
As regards family members, the more you come to the care home to visit, the less likely will abuse be. If you can't go yourself, send a friend or an advocate. An advocate can be a volunteer, perhaps from a religious group if the resident is religious. If you can't visit because you live far away and no-one else can, you should seriously consider moving your relative to a care home near you.

When you visit, ask to see the care plan and daily care logs. It is your legal right to have access to them, so if you are denied access, you should start thinking that there is something fishy with the care home and you should consider investigating what dark reasons there might be behind barring you from reading the care records.

Once you gain access to the care plan and daily logs, you should make sure that the care plan has been updated and that it still describes your relative's needs accurately. As regards daily care logs, watch out for short entries that don't mean anything such as "Care given". Also, cut and paste should be easy to spot. This happens when carers write exactly the same entries every day. Another thing to watch out for is log entries written by someone who did not provide the care. This is often done on behalf of carers who forget to log the care entry. Only if you notice and point out these things, the care notes will reflect accurately what sort of support your relative received. This way you will also be doing the care home a favour by helping to raise their care standards.

Physical abuse
Ripped clothes are a tell-tell sign of rough handling, which is a type of physical abuse. If, after buying stretchy clothes for your relative, you still find that some of their clothes are ripped, you'll have to investigate further and perhaps even put a hidden camera in their room.

Reflection points and positive advice you can offer to carers and managers

1. Understaffing.

Managers are bound by the *Good governance* care standard (Regulation 17) to implement systems and processes in order to guarantee the quality and constant improvement of the services they provide. There are many things a care home can do to this end, for example hiring a professional manager, someone who understands what it is to lead teams of people. A manager needs to be on the floor both to supervise and to give moral support to staff. There is nothing worse for workers than feeling that there is no leadership, especially during busy times. No one is better placed to enforce standards than someone in higher authority. This sends an important zero tolerance message as regards cutting corners. Presence of high management on the floor also gives care coordinators and other leaders the support they need when faced with maintaining high standards of care.

Hiring the best workers, as suggested by the care standards in *Fit and proper persons employed* (Regulation 19), and improving team building and staff rapport would also help avoid rough handling of vulnerable clients. Teams of carers who like each other work well together, are more efficient, and they are likely to do a better job of time management.

An incentives programme for carers, including rewards and career opportunities, would also help managers improve performance and raise care standards.

2. Intimidating over-empowered carers.

This is partly answered in point 1 above: management presence on the floor is key here in order to nip malpractice in the bud once it is spotted. Insisting on a zero tolerance policy is important, so if a new employee reports misconduct or malpractice, everyone should know that the allegations will be taken seriously.

3. Clothing that does not fit

Family members should buy stretchy clothes and clothes a size bigger. This could even be made into a mandatory home policy on the grounds that the policy is protecting clients from rough handling.

4. Safeguarding service users from abuse and improper treatment when care happens behind closed doors.

This question is answered in point 1 above. The manager needs to be visible. Their presence and authority must be felt and seen by everyone. If getting more staff on the floor is out of the question and you are forced to send your carers on an impossible mission, they should at least have a strong leader to guide them and make sure they follow agreed ways of working. Needless to say, one does not need to be a tyrant in order to assert authority and guide teams.

5. New carers working with senior staff who don't follow agreed ways of working.

A new carer might learn that ignoring agreed ways of working is fine. They might also be responsible for any malpractice taking place while working with a senior carer who does not follow policy. Therefore, rogue practices should be rooted out as soon as they are found.

6. *'Is this really happening?'* The tall carer is so shocked by the rough handling that he goes into a denial of what is happening right before his own eyes.

The shock is the cause of the denial, but the root of the problem lies in the tall carer not having expected to find problems in the first place. Other professions including police officers, military personnel, prison officers and even teachers can face shock and denial when confronted by distressing situations. Psychological shock is also called *acute stress reaction*, *acute stress disorder* or *emotional shock* and it can be followed by denial of the trigger event among other symptoms. Anyone experiencing such shock needs to seek counselling. The first port of call is your line manager. Also, the Royal College of Nursing offers affordable full membership for carers including free counselling and legal advice.

7. The carers are faced with a dilemma when the room floor is covered in faeces. According to Health and Safety regulations in any place of training, what is more urgent: to clean the mess on the floor first so it does not spread everywhere (including the carers shoes and clothes), or to help the client?

According to Health and Safety regulations, in a care setting the safety and health of workers comes first. But, in this case, there are two workers, so one could have taken care of the safety of the client while the other one took care of hygiene.

8. Taking into account the fact that Harry is non-responsive, should a stand aid have been used in this situation?

Brutal Care

It seems that Harry was having a bad day since he was not responsive and couldn't support his own weight. The carers should have called someone in leadership in order to obtain permission to use a hoist instead.

9. What other standards and/or codes of practice have been broken? Think about the tall carer's attitude, for example.

The tall carer should have stood up to the senior carer and should even have reported the rough handling taking place. All carers are bound to a *duty of care* as laid out by the care standards and the codes of conduct. Please refer to the accompanying appendices.

This Is Not Happening

A carer has called in sick and we are short staffed again[5]. A long list of residents to wake up, wash, dress and take to the dining room in time for breakfast. It is essential to prioritise when you only have two hours to do all that. One or two residents will have to have breakfast in bed. My partner and I will have to split and work alone, and maybe help each other with the transfers, with the hoisting and the stand aid.

The tall carer in the polo shirt has been learning the ropes and now understands that being nice to people and giving them the time they need to wake up and wash and get dressed at their own pace is not what care in a care home is all about. It is rather about time management. So, when he heard that they were short, he skipped the briefing with the nurse and the other carers and went straight to Richard, gave him a quick shave and a shower, helped him into his clothes, made his bed and brought him a cup of tea.

20 minutes flat. A good head start. Great. And now, to Elsie.

Elsie is not what we call a *'single'*. She needs two carers, especially with the hoisting from bed to her wheelchair; but the tall man has agreed with his partner to split in order to speed up the shift. *We'll see how this goes. Elsie is all right with me. She'll be all right.*[6]

The man knocks on the door and walks in carrying towels, bed sheets, wipes, and gloves.

'Good morning, Elsie! How are you today?'

He turns on the light and walks closer to the bed.

'Hello, Elsie! Good morning. How are you?' he repeats a bit louder.

---

[5] **Care Standards**: *18. Staffing.* (1) Sufficient numbers of suitably qualified, competent, skilled and experienced persons must be deployed in order to meet the requirements of this Part.

[6] **Care Standards:** *10. Dignity and respect.* (1) Service users must be treated with dignity and respect. (2) Without limiting paragraph (1), the things which a registered person is required to do to comply with paragraph (1) include in particular— (a) ensuring the privacy of the service user.
13. Safeguarding service users from abuse and improper treatment. (1) Service users must be protected from abuse and improper treatment in accordance with this regulation. (2) Systems and processes must be established and operated effectively to prevent abuse of service users.

©Alex Matthews 2018

Elsie is responding. Her back muscles push up a few inches and she goes flat on her back again. Too much effort first thing in the morning. A faint hello leaves her lips.

'Elsie, I'll put your hearing aid in. Alright?'

A nod for an answer. Not a normal nod, but one that takes great effort to put into motion.

'Is that better, Elsie? It is just me today, Elsie. Donna will be here later to help me transfer you to your wheelchair. Is that alright?'
'You do what you have to do. Don't mind me.'[7]

Elsie's responses have become mantras that she can safely repeat in any situation. *'That will be all right. If you think so. Don't mind me. You know what you are doing. I'm such a bother to you. I'm stupid.'* But what the carer is concerned with now is Elsie's stiffness. On a previous shift working together, Donna, a senior carer, had explained that Elsie hadn't been as rigid and scared when she first came to the home. *'Rough handling, apparently. She spent a whole morning crying once. Someone did something to her, poor thing. That's why we have to use a hoist with a full sling now. She's not safe anymore.'*

The man carefully chooses some clothes for Elsie.

'Is this alright for today? Nice top. You have some nice clothes, Elsie. Is it all right to start your personal care?'

'Don't mind me. You know what you are doing.'

The duvet goes up in the air and a collection of bones is revealed under a pink nightie. The carer places a bath towel on Elsie's legs in order to preserve her dignity. He then hands Elsie a flannel with warm water so she can wash her face.

'Well done. We need to remove your nightie now, Elsie. Could you lean forward, please?'

Elsie seems happy to oblige. She is looking at the carer now. Is she smiling? The carer examines Elsie's eyes. She really is settled. That's a relief. He washes and dresses Elsie's top half first. Clean flannel, soapy warm water

---

[7] **Code of Conduct 2:** *Promote and uphold the privacy, dignity, rights, health and wellbeing of people who use health and care services and their carers at all times.* 6. always maintain the privacy and dignity of people who use health and care services, their carers and others.

©Alex Matthews 2018

and moisturiser. Elsie is not stiff today. She is actually co-operating. Lifting her back a bit, moving her legs and arms to let the carer give her a proper wash. Now he washes her legs, and slips on clean underwear and a pair of slacks, but not all the way up.

'Thank you, Elsie. I now need to remove your pad and make you clean. Is that all right?'

'Yes, yes. You go ahead. I'm so sorry. I'm such a bother to you.'

'No, Elsie. You are alright.'

He really wishes he didn't have to do this part alone, but this is what time management is about. He hates that term, *'time management'*, a pseudonym; management speak for *'do a quick job and get out'*. Doing things the right way and with more staff would take longer. That would drive the price of care up and no one would be able to afford it then. What a dilemma. *There must be care homes where things are done the right way*, he wonders. *I should find out and apply for a job there, because this is beginning to be too much for me.* And before he can even think about resigning from his job and find the perfect care home, Elsie's sacral area is clean, the pad is on and she is ready for the transfer to her wheelchair.

'Thank you. Thank you very much. I don't know how you can do that. The things I make you do. I am so useless.'

'No problem, Elsie. Glad to help. You deserve it. We just need to wait for Donna now. She'll help us transfer you to your wheelchair.'

But Elsie is smiling and moving on the bed. Is she really going to sit up by herself? The carer is finishing tidying up the room and worrying that Elsie might fall off the bed.

'Careful, Elsie. Are you alright?'

But Elsie is very all right. She is moving at snail's pace towards the edge of the bed and the carer cannot believe it. He quickly lowers the bed. Elsie knows what she is doing. She is now safely sitting on the edge of the bed, looking at her wheelchair.

Oh, dear. According to her care plan, we cannot attempt any transfers without a hoist. But this is what she wants to do. Who am I to limit her mobility. And I cannot restrain her either, that would infringe her basic human rights.

©Alex Matthews 2018

This Is Not Happening

The carer moves the wheelchair nearer to the bed, within Elsie's reach, and puts the brakes on.

I'm not doing this! I am just putting the wheelchair here because Elsie wants to stand. I'm sure she is not going to turn and sit on it. She just wants to stand and stretch her legs. It's been ages since she last stood up. Morning exercise, that's all. But if the nurse happens to come in now, I'll be in so much trouble. If Elsie were to fall, it would be my fault. They would take me to court. I am liable. This is not happening!

The carer is really hoping that no one comes in, not even Donna, because Elsie is standing up facing the chair and it looks as if she is going to attempt a turn and sit down. She is almost there. She is taking ages, but she is doing it. She is able. She is turning into the chair.

We haven't taken away her mobility completely. A miracle!

The carer is close to Elsie, his arms outstretched lest she should fall. Elsie still smiling, showing him that she is not useless. Just then, Donna storms into the room, advances (not very surprised at the miracle) and shoves Elsie into the wheelchair[8].

'It was her idea entirely!', exclaims the carer rather sheepishly in his own defence. But Donna couldn't care less about the Moving and Handling policy

---

[8] **Code of Conduct 2:** *Promote and uphold the privacy, dignity, rights, health and wellbeing of people who use health and care services and their carers at all times.*
As a Healthcare Support Worker or Adult Social Care Worker in England you must:
1. always act in the best interests of people who use health and care services.
2. always treat people with respect and compassion.
3. put the needs, goals and aspirations of people who use health and care services first, helping them to be in control and to choose the healthcare, care and support they receive.
4. promote people's independence and ability to self-care, assisting those who use health and care services to exercise their rights and make informed choices.
5. always gain valid consent before providing healthcare, care and support. You must also respect a person's right to refuse to receive healthcare, care and support if they are capable of doing so.
6. always maintain the privacy and dignity of people who use health and care services, their carers and others.
7. be alert to any changes that could affect a person's needs or progress and report your observations in line with your employer's agreed ways of working.
8. always make sure that your actions or omissions do not harm an individual's health or wellbeing. You must never abuse, neglect, harm or exploit those who use health and care services, their carers or your colleagues.
9. challenge and report dangerous, abusive, discriminatory or exploitative behaviour or practice.

©Alex Matthews 2018

or legal liabilities. She just wants to get on with the shift and is now heading for the door with Elsie.

'Well done! We are doing well this morning. We are going to be alright. I'll take Elsie to breakfast.'

And off they go into the corridor, the wheelchair breaking speed limits. *Good bye, Elsie. Time is all we needed to succeed. I failed you when you needed someone to stand up for you against inhumane policies, liability, and brutal carers. I am so sorry, Elsie. I am the useless one, not you.*[9]

---

[9] **Care Standards:** *13. Safeguarding service users from abuse and improper treatment.* (1) Service users must be protected from abuse and improper treatment in accordance with this regulation. (2) Systems and processes must be established and operated effectively to prevent abuse of service users.

This is not happening

Main point of advice

Institutional abuse

This story shows how policy and avoiding liabilities take preference over person centred care. Unfortunately, this increases the risk of service users getting institutionalised and turned into invalids, and there is very little one can do about it. Even the most expensive care homes do not have gyms nor do they employ physiotherapists. Also, as it is evident in this story, carers hardly have the time to carry out the most basic care needs, so forget about them getting people moving and exercising. It is therefore important that you learn how to give your relative their physiotherapy on a regular basis. As it was advised in the previous chapter, visiting frequently is an essential part of providing your relative the care they deserve. Care homes can only fulfill the most basic care needs: personal care, nutrition and medication. Everything else, from physiotherapy, to psychological needs, to socialising is left to the relatives; to you. Residents who get regular visits exercise the most. Human beings need more than just personal care, food and medication. You'll need to be there to provide all these other things for your relative.

Reflection points and positive advice you can offer to carers and managers

1. The phrases 'he'll be alright' and 'she'll be alright' are often used by carers in care homes to mean that a given resident will have to go without the care they need.

When someone says that a client *'will'* be all right, they obviously imply that the client is not all right. When someone is all right, we say *'she is all right'* or *'she said that she was all right'*. Saying that someone *will* be all right with the intention of not giving them the care they need contravenes the person centred care standard (Regulation 9) as well as the second code of conduct. Please refer to accompanying appendices.

2. The tall carer is faced with an impossible dilemma. If you gave each resident the time they needed, care would become even more expensive and no one would be able to afford it.

Perhaps this is an impossible conundrum, but looking at care homes where things are done correctly as well as at how care is organised in other

©Alex Matthews 2018

countries could help shed some light on the answer. For example, some Spanish care homes rely on relatives and volunteers to lend a hand with the social aspects of care such as conversation, taking residents for walks and making cups of coffee for them. There are also official volunteer organizations (the Spanish Red Cross among them) who train volunteers to do other more complex tasks such as helping with meals and taking clients on outings or to the hospital.

3. Why is the tall carer so surprised at the fact that Elsie can *still* move independently? Do policy and regulation really take away people's mobility? Are care homes turning people into invalids for the sake of avoiding falls and accidents?

When more relatives and volunteers are available to help with the simple tasks, carers have more time to help people with their mobility. Employing volunteers is already being done in some UK care homes and in other countries. Efforts could be increased so the practice is more widespread.

4. The tall carer missed an important handover session with the nurse and the other carers. Why? Is the tall carer following agreed ways of working? What seems to be happening to the tall carer? Think about the kind of pressure he is under and the transformation he is going through.

The tall carer is making his own rules. In fact, he seems to be yielding to the huge pressure to get everyone ready before breakfast and turning into a rogue carer in the process. What's worrying is that he can actually get away with it, which reveals an underlying management problem.

5. Was it all right for the carers to split and work individually in order to speed up the shift?

The carers were not following agreed ways of working. They violated several care standards and statements in the Code of Conduct, in particular Code 3: *Work in collaboration with your colleagues to ensure the delivery of high quality, safe and compassionate healthcare, care and support.*

6. Regulation and policy sometimes clash with people's rights and wishes. Which is right in this situation: To let Elsie move independently and sit in the wheelchair, or restrain her for her own safety?

Whatever you do in this situation is going to be wrong. This kind of dilemma is fairly common in a heavily regulated sector such as the care industry. If you restrain Elsie for her own safety, you are violating her basic human rights. If you let her move independently she might fall and even die as a result of the fall.

7. Why is the tall carer so frustrated in the last paragraph?

The tall carer is frustrated at not being able to give his clients the time they need in order to perform at their best. He is also failing to stand up for his clients against abuse and that makes him feel a fraud.

Tom's Hand

The old man goes on his knees and lies on one side on the corridor floor. He adopts a foetal position and closes his eyes. His one-to-one carer fetches a cushion and places it carefully under his head.

Tom is having a very difficult time today. He refused to have a shower when he got up, and getting him washed and dressed was a challenge for his carer. He managed to walk half way to the dining room for breakfast, but had to be taken the rest of the way on a wheelchair. During breakfast, he wasn't able to aim the spoon at his mouth, using his hands to grab his fried food at times. He had to be fed while his spoon moved full of imaginary food from the plate to his mouth. He then fell asleep at the table. When he woke up twenty minutes later, some of the other residents were still having breakfast. He pulled violently at his bib with a determination in his eyes that evidenced his state of mind. His one-to-one helped Tom loosen his apron. Tom then stood up with some difficulty, stumbling, pulling at the table cloth and moving straight for the other residents' chairs.

'Tom, I'm sorry but I can't let you shake people like that.'

Tom's one-to-one knows well that Tom can only be restrained if he poses a threat to himself or other people. And now he was posing a threat. Tom is a strong, heavy man, though, with the arms of a bricklayer. The carer tried a mix of pleading and soft pushing with invitations to sit on the nearby sofa at the other end of the dining room. But the devil had got the better of Tom and he now made for the fire extinguisher on the wall. Being subtle about restraining Tom was not working. Unwillingly, the carer had to wrestle the heavy object from Tom's grasp and lead him with both hands all the way to the sofa. He hated to be forceful with Tom like that. Tom sat for a while, closed his eyes and let his carer help clear the breakfast tables and the mess on the floor.

But Tom's naps never lasted very long. Soon he was trying to stand up, still the stern look on his face, and off he went stumbling along the corridor, his carer by his side. Tom then entered some of the bedrooms. Nothing his carer or anybody else could do about it. For, as long as he wasn't shaking people about, he could not be stopped. After his little tour of the bedrooms and an inspection of the walls, doors and the hand rail, he decided it was time to check the strength of the work by banging on the walls. Everything was all right. Or not all right. The building was good. Or maybe not.

You were so in love, weren't you. You had it all, Tom. A proud self-made man, you put up with postwar hardships, started as a labourer and paid for

©Alex Matthews 2018

your own education. You had a beautiful family, holidays in foreign countries, a business, a reputation, and the most precious thing of all, you had love. But it was all taken away from you in the cruellest of ways. You used to fall asleep at her bedside, sometimes on the floor, as you are doing now. You nursed her until nothing was left of her. And then this, no speech, no balance, no memory. She is here, is she not, right now? She is always near you.

Now Ivy is looking at you with anguished eyes.

'Well, isn't anybody going to do anything about it? Help the poor man!'

'He is fine, Ivy. This is what he wants to do. We have to respect his choices.'

'But can't you see that he is suffering? You can't leave him there on the floor. This isn't how you treat a human being.'

'Ivy, I can assure you that Tom is safe. He'll be up in a minute, when he is ready. He does this all the time.'

'Oh, I'll say! This is disgraceful. If you won't do anything about it, I will.'

And saying this, Ivy lets go of her walking frame and starts lowering herself towards Tom. The carer in the polo shirt can't believe his bad luck. He put in a fifteen hour shift yesterday and he is still really exhausted.

'Please, Ivy, you are going to injure yourself. Please, don't!' he pleads making a gesture to stop Ivy from interfering. At this point, Ivy breaks down in tears of indignation. *What a day you are giving me, Tom,* the carer thinks. *This is just what I needed!* At this point, a nurse becomes aware of the big fuss in the corridor and takes Ivy away. As was expected, Tom is back and trying to stand up. But... *Oh, no!*

'Not here, Tom. We are in a public place, Tom. I can't let you do that. We can go to the toilet just there, look.'

But the spirit of the self-made man is strong. His trousers are going down. *I will not be broken. I'm still here.* His carer now calls for a wheelchair. Tom likes to be taken around in a wheelchair. Perhaps he feels he's going somewhere. Indeed, the sight of the chair and the presence of the other carer distract Tom from whatever it was he had wanted to do. Enough with the trouble, Tom will have to go to his room now. He needs a pad change and he needs to relax. Sometimes, being in his room makes him feel less agitated.

But his carer is wrong. As soon as they arrive in the room, Tom stands up and grabs the arm chair in the corner dragging it all the way to the en suite bathroom door. His carer knows that this is not the right time, but he also knows that he must try several times before he can get consent, and this will be the first. Strangely, Tom agrees to go into the bathroom for a pad change. It needs to be a really fast and efficient operation. With Tom in this mood, anything can happen. *Gosh, this job can be stressful. If I could only close my eyes for a few minutes.* As expected, as soon as the trousers are down and the pad is off, Tom starts urinating in the bathroom waste bin. *At least it isn't the bedroom carpet.* A few fast moves and a clean pad is on and the trousers are up. The challenge now is to convince Tom to rest for a while and we are in luck, because he comes out of the bathroom and sinks into the armchair. *At last! It is so hot here!* And, as the tall man in the polo shirt turns towards the fan, bang goes Tom against the bathroom door.

It doesn't look serious. The door has broken the fall and Tom hasn't hit the floor hard. He seems a bit shocked by the fall. *How did that happen? He was just sitting there.* The one-to-one calls for help. Tom is not moving. By the time the nurse arrives, Tom is already coming to and he seems to be fine. But he's not. There is blood all over his right hand. A big skin tear. They help Tom into his armchair and the nurse runs to get her kit.

'Oh, dear, how did this happen?' she asks when she returns. 'This is so bad. You have to be more careful. That's why he has a one-to-one, so these things can be avoided.'

The carer explains that Tom was sitting down, that he must have thrashed himself off the chair. The nurse cleans the wound in the most squeamish way possible and applies a large dressing almost turning the other way while she continues with her reprimand.

'Look at him, this is disgraceful. Now, watch him carefully.'

But the carer is beyond fatigue now[10]. He can only think, *If I could close my eyes just for a few minutes.* Fortunately, Tom shuts his eyes and seems settled. *Great, this is my chance to rest a bit. What a day!* The man in the polo shirt grabs a chair and a newspaper. He closes his eyes for a minute and then glances at Tom. *Still sleeping, great.* He closes his eyes for another minute, then looks at Tom again. Still sleeping. And he repeats this a few times until the nurse returns to check on Tom.

---

[10] **Care Standards:** *19. Fit and proper persons employed.* (1) [...] (c) be able by reason of their health, after reasonable adjustments are made, of properly performing tasks which are intrinsic to the work for which they are employed.
Code of Conduct 2: *Promote and uphold the privacy, dignity, rights, health and wellbeing of people who use health and care services and their carers at all times.*

©Alex Matthews 2018

'What's this? Look at him!'

Tom has blood all over his hand. The carer is both embarrassed and fed up and doesn't want to say anything.

'I was watching him.'

But he had a newspaper in his hand and anything could happen now. He could even be accused of neglect. No point in saying that he hadn't been reading the newspaper. That he had been looking at Tom's face and he seemed asleep.

'It wasn't his face you had to watch, it was his hand. Please, get out of here.'

Good bye, Tom. I let you down. I am so sorry. I was honoured to take care of you for quite a long time. You called me my son when you saw me arrive. You smiled at me when you were back from the dark places. I prayed for you and I held your hand. You are lucky to be so dangerous.

Tom's Hand

Main point of advice

Long hours
Carers work long hours and you can expect them to be very tired and prone to making mistakes. One thing that carers appreciate is to have volunteers and relatives around the home taking care of simple tasks such as helping residents to eat and drink, taking them for walks, drawing their curtains, changing TV channels for them, and even passing messages on to the carers when a more complex need arises, such as a pad change. If you can't visit often, you should at least try to find a friend, a befriender, or a volunteer who could spend time with your relative and lessen the burden on the carers. These can be found through dedicated charities such as Age UK, or through a faith group.

Reflection points and positive advice you can offer to carers and managers

1. Consequences of working long hours.

Everyone knows that mistakes are made when people are tired. It becomes difficult to concentrate and focus on the task at hand. This means that if we make staff work fifteen-hour shifts, we are putting our clients at risk. This directly contravenes safeguarding standards.

2. What can leaders do in order to support carers when they are tired?

If making staff work long hours cannot be avoided, a manager should make sure to assign less demanding tasks to those who are suffering from fatigue. In this case study, the tall carer has to deal with challenging behaviour even though he is still really exhausted from his long shift of the previous day.

3. What can leaders do to support carers who have to deal with their clients' challenging behaviour?

Staff need special training in order to deal with challenging behaviour. This training should include self-defence. Carers might be asked to 'lend a hand' with dementia care. They need to be ready for this and know that they have a right to specific training before they are asked to work in dementia care.

©Alex Matthews 2018

4. When taking care of dementia sufferers with challenging behaviour, carers need to think on their feet and come up with the best possible course of action while taking into account policy, agreed ways of working, standards and the code of conduct. What are some examples of on-the-spot decisions from this case study?

The tall carer decided that a shower would not be possible so he opted for a wash instead. The carer had to get a wheelchair for Tom because he had stopped walking half way to the dining room. Then he decided to help Tom eat as he didn't seem able to do it by himself on this particular occasion. The tall carer also let Tom have a nap at the breakfast table. The carer then had to wrestle a fire extinguisher from his client's grasp. The carer also let Tom go into other residents' rooms, and lie on the floor when he needed it. The tall carer managed to stop his client from pulling his pants down in a public place. And he managed to tend to his client's toilet needs fairly successfully. In order to make these informed decisions, the tall carer had to take into account the home's restraining policy, the European Human Rights Charter, the Fundamental Care Standards and the Code of Conduct. And, of course, his previous knowledge of his client, including all the confidential information in the client's care plan.

5. The nurse wasn't particularly sympathetic or understanding towards the tall carer. Do you think it was only the carer's fault that Tom scratched his dressing? Could the nurse have done anything to prevent Tom from scratching his dressing?

The tall carer was definitely in the wrong, but he had been handling Tom's challenging behaviour since early in the morning. Perhaps the nurse could have given him a break instead of a reprimand. Also, as a more experienced member of staff, she should have anticipated that Tom would scratch his dressing and she could have warned the carer about it.

6. Why does the tall carer say to Tom *'you are lucky to be so dangerous'*?

Tom is lucky because challenging dementia sufferers are often assigned one-to-one carers. Dementia sufferers who are not challenging spend very long hours just sitting by themselves with no one to interact with.

Elsie's Men

Elsie is pushed in her wheelchair by a big man in black trousers and a blue polo shirt. Behind follows another big man edging a hoist carefully along the corridor. Elsie doesn't talk to the men. *A bit more slowly, please. Why did you take so long to take me to my room? I'm so tired*[11], are all left unsaid. There is a lump in her throat. There is always a lump in her throat.[12]

The home is almost too quiet this time of day, an hour or so after the evening meal. Most residents are already in bed. All is quiet except for in Elsie's bedroom.

'What's that banging on the wall?'

'It's the radiator. It's broken. I tried to turn it off earlier, but it really is broken. The maintenance people will have to check it tomorrow[13]*.'*

'I didn't realise a radiator could make that kind of noise. It sounds like someone hammering the wall.'

The man in the polo shirt checks the radiator in disbelief. The noise is really coming from the radiator.

'I can't believe this. Anyway, we shouldn't be working together. I mean, two men are not allowed to work together.'[14]

---

[11] **Care Standards**: *9. Person-centred care*. (1) The care and treatment of service users must (a) be appropriate, (b) meet their needs, and (c) reflect their preferences. **Code of Conduct 2**: Promote and uphold the privacy, dignity, rights, health and wellbeing of people who use health and care services and their carers at all times.

[12] **Care Standards**: *11. Need for consent*. (1) Care and treatment of service users must only be provided with the consent of the relevant person.
Code of Conduct 2, as above.

[13] **Care Standards**: *15. Premises and equipment*. All premises and equipment used by the service provider must be […] (e) properly maintained.

[14] **Care Standards**: *10 Dignity and respect*. (c) having due regard to any relevant protected characteristics (as defined in section 149(7) of the Equality Act 2010) of the service user. The relevant protected characteristics are age; disability; gender reassignment; pregnancy and maternity; race; religion or belief; sex; sexual orientation).
Care Standards: *13. Safeguarding service users from abuse and improper treatment*.
Code of Conduct 2: Promote and uphold the privacy, dignity, rights, health and wellbeing of people who use health and care services and their carers at all times. 6. always maintain the privacy and dignity of people who use health and care services, their carers and others. And 9. challenge and report dangerous, abusive,

'I don't know where Kim is[15]. Besides, Elsie needs to go to bed. She is exhausted. She'll be alright.'[16]

Elsie is arranged in the middle of the poorly lit room. The two men kindly explain to her what is about to follow. A heavy machine faces Elsie.

'Is it alright to get you ready for bed, Elsie? I mean, do you mind us being men?'

'No, you do what you have to do. Oh, I am so silly. I am such a bother.'

Both men reassure Elsie that she is not a bother; that she is going to be fine. After getting her top clothes off, the men slip a nightie on the skinny body. A blue sling is pressed tightly around her back and latched onto the metallic arms of the hoist.

'We are going up, Elsie.'

The machine lifts Elsie, wrapped in her cocoon, first up and into the air, swinging slightly then down onto the bed. Elsie knows the motions, so she sits up a little, just enough to let the men get the sling out of the way.

'Thank you, Elsie. Sorry, we need to pull these down. We are going to give you a freshen-up.'

'That's all right. I'm so silly. Don't mind me. You do what you have to do.'

But Elsie has been sitting in faeces for a few hours since her last pad change and these have moved up and now sit, like set clay, all over the front of her pelvis.[17]

---

discriminatory or exploitative behaviour or practice.

[15] **Care Standards**: *18. Staffing.* (1) Sufficient numbers of suitably qualified, competent, skilled and experienced persons must be deployed in order to meet the requirements of this Part.

[16] **Care Standards**: *9 Person-centred care*. 1.c. as above.
Code of Conduct 2: 3. put the needs, goals and aspirations of people who use health and care services first, helping them to be in control and to choose the healthcare, care and support they receive.
4. promote people's independence and ability to self-care, assisting those who use health and care services to exercise their rights and make informed choices.

[17] **Care Standards**: *12. Safe care and treatment.* (1) Care and treatment must be provided in a safe way for service users. […] (2) Without limiting paragraph (1), the things which a registered person must do to comply with that paragraph include: (a) assessing the risks to the health and safety of service users of receiving the care or treatment; (b) doing all that is reasonably practicable to mitigate any such risks; […]

'I've never seen anything like it!'

'I'll bet the back is clean.'

'Oh, I'm such a silly old fool. I'm such a nuisance!'

'Don't worry, Elsie. We are going to clean it up. You'll be feeling dry and comfortable in no time.'

'We should be giving her a shower, really, but, at this time of the night…'

'We'll use plenty of soapy water. We'll have to change the bed afterwards.'

'Oh, I'm bad. I'm useless.'

'No, Elsie, this kind of thing happens all the time. Don't you worry. Soon, you'll be feeling clean and comfortable.'

A clean pair of pants cannot be found in Elsie's chest of draws, so one of the men needs to run to the laundry room to fetch clean underwear. If two men are not supposed to work together, what do our policies say about a single man providing care for a lady? wonders the tall man in the polo shirt. He starts pouring warm soapy water on the faeces in order to soften and loosen them.

'Sorry, Elsie, I need to do this.'

But the job isn't easy. The faeces have formed a kind of hard adobe with the pubic hair. More warm water is needed to loosen it. More embarrassment. More kind words. More rubbing with a flannel. Good job the home has run

---

(h) assessing the risk of, and preventing, detecting and controlling the spread of, infections, including those that are health care associated; (i) where responsibility for the care and treatment of service users is shared with, or transferred to, other persons, working with such other persons, service users and other appropriate persons to ensure that timely care planning takes place to ensure the health, safety and welfare of the service users.

Code of Conduct 2: *Promote and uphold the privacy, dignity, rights, health and wellbeing of people who use health and care services and their carers at all times.*
7. be alert to any changes that could affect a person's needs or progress and report your observations in line with your employer's agreed ways of working.
8. always make sure that your actions or omissions do not harm an individual's health or wellbeing. You must never abuse, neglect, harm or exploit those who use health and care services, their carers or your colleagues.
9. challenge and report dangerous, abusive, discriminatory or exploitative behaviour or practice.

©Alex Matthews 2018

out of wipes[18]. A flannel is better at scouring all this stuff off. By the time the other man arrives with the underwear, Elsie is so flushed and embarrassed she has gone completely silent. She is dirty and silly and a bother. Scared and helpless too.

The two men make Elsie comfortable in bed and offer kind words of reassurance again before disappearing into the silent corridors. Thump, thump, thump. The noisy radiator will keep Elsie company for the whole night.

'Wasn't she supposed to get a pad change in the afternoon?'

'I don't know. I thought Kim had done it.'

'I wouldn't be able to sleep with that racket going on. Poor thing.'

---

[18] **Care Standards**: *15. Premises and equipment.* (1) All premises and equipment used by the service provider must be (a) clean, (b) secure, (c) suitable for the purpose for which they are being used, (d) properly used (e) properly maintained, and (f) appropriately located for the purpose for which they are being used.
(2) The registered person must, in relation to such premises and equipment, maintain standards of hygiene appropriate for the purposes for which they are being used.

©Alex Matthews 2018

Elsie's Men

Main point of advice

Personal hygiene

Elsie spent the whole afternoon and evening without a pad change. She was sitting on a soiled pad for a very long time. This is an example of institutional abuse, which happens when the organizational needs are put before the needs of the individual. In this case we are talking about understaffing leading to neglect. Neglect itself is also a form of abuse. Therefore, it could be argued that institutional abuse leads to all kinds of collateral malpractice. So, how can you make sure that your relative's hygiene needs are taken care of properly? You will need to inspect your relative's bedsheets for stains, make sure the towels in their bathroom are clean, check your relative's clothes for stains, make sure they are wearing their own clothes and not someone else's. If possible, ask for your relative to be put on a continence chart, so you can see how often they get a pad change. I will never tire of saying that when family members are involved in the care of their relative, the sort of support that the relative receives from the care team is much better than that of residents who have no advocates.

Reflection points and positive advice you can offer to carers and managers

1. In this particular care home, two men are not supposed to give care to a lady. Why?

In many establishments, including National Health Service hospitals, two male health care professionals are allowed to work together. One can only guess that the idea behind banning two male carers from working together in this particular nursing home is to avoid service users from unnecessary worry. It must be quite embarrassing for a lady to be alone with two men while they take care of her personal hygiene. In this case, the care home is trying to safeguard the clients. But, basically, when there are no female carers available, the resident needs to choose between male carers or no care, so she has no real choice. In this case, the home is in breach of its own policies and several fundamental care standards.

2. If two men are not allowed to give care to a lady, should a single man be allowed?

In this nursing home, two male carers are not allowed to work together, but a single male carer is allowed to work alone and give hygiene care to female clients providing they don't object. This is really not consistent with the idea of safeguarding clients from the worry of being alone with male carers when hygiene care is given.

3. How can residents get timely pad changes?

A schedule for pad checks and changes should be implemented for each client, where carers record when the pad was checked or changed.

4. What can a leader do in order protect clients from discomfort or harm from building maintenance?

A leader needs to be on the floor as much as possible. There are many small details of maintenance that can add to the discomfort of the residents, such as doors that don't shut properly, lights that don't work, or faulty beds. These problems are usually noticed by carers and nurses and logged in a maintenance log book, but considering the example given in this case study, someone in authority should be available at all times to decide if a maintenance job needs to be done urgently.

5. Why is Kim not around to help?

It looks as if the nursing home is short staffed again, which contravenes the fundamental standard on Staffing (Regulation 18). Kim is probably taking a break, or she could be helping the nurse in one of the rooms. Whatever the reason, we can see a communication problem here too as the other two male carers don't know where she is.

6. Why is one of the carers not sure about whether Kim had changed Elsie's pad in the afternoon?

There is a communication problem here, which violates the third code of conduct: *Work in collaboration with your colleagues to ensure the delivery of high quality, safe and compassionate healthcare, care and support.* No one was sure whether Elsie had had a pad change, which resulted in Elsie sitting in a soiled pad for hours, followed by a gruelling personal hygiene session.

Pyjama Party

There is a pyjama party at the home tonight and the tall carer has been invited. There is going to be a fair deal of pushing people about, rolling them in their sleep, throwing pads in the air and walking from room to room without a change of gloves. The tall carer has just been asked to stay on and help with the night shift. It is going to be his first time on this shift and he has no idea about the party, so he's in for a surprise.

Another day's work is over. Most residents are in bed. All the carers have left except for the party goer. The tall carer is introduced to André, the smiley mountain of muscles he will be working with. Two men working together again[19], but at least André looks friendly.

André prepares a trolley with pads, towels and everything they will need. There are usually only two carers on the night shift and quite a lot to do. Most residents will get a pad change before midnight and a few of them will need repositioning, so the huge man is very grateful for the help.

'We'll start at the top and work our way down,' he explains as the tall carer stands by waiting for instructions.

Indeed, the night shift is so different the tall carer is at a loss as to how to help. In fact, he wonders if they have different policies for the night shift but, before he has a chance to take it all in, they are entering rooms without as much as a knock. They move stealthily under the cover of darkness and proceed to break the rest of the home's policies.

André is so strong he can roll people with what seems to be a flick. Before the tall carer can even think about it, wet pads are out on the carpet, dry ones are on and all without a wash, without a word of warning[20]. Some residents are startled out of sleep and mutter some loosely connected words. Others don't even wake up. The pads go into a yellow bag outside in

---

[19] **Care Standards:** *10. Dignity and respect.* (1) Service users must be treated with dignity and respect. (2) Without limiting paragraph (1), the things which a registered person is required to do to comply with paragraph (1) include in particular— (a) ensuring the privacy of the service user; (b) supporting the autonomy, independence and involvement in the community of the service user; (c) having due regard to any relevant protected characteristics (as defined in section 149(7) of the Equality Act 2010) of the service user.

[20] **Care Standards:** *11. Need for consent.* (1) Care and treatment of service users must only be provided with the consent of the relevant person.

©Alex Matthews 2018

the trolley. A few residents have had a pad change already, but André hasn't changed his gloves yet[21].

The tall carer feels that this is all wrong and questions André, but André is very friendly and answers with a big smile. *'It's alright. Don't worry about it, it's night time.'* All the rules, the standard procedure, don't seem to apply at night. Consent is not obtained from residents, the moving and handling seems to be inspired by martial arts, hygiene is out of the window. But what would be the point in reporting all this malpractice when the nurse is watching and doesn't say a word[22]. It is evident that this is how a standard night shift is organised. So the tall carer decides to let André carry on.

---

[21] **Care Standards:** *12. Safe care and treatment.* (1) Care and treatment must be provided in a safe way for service users.
Code of Conduct 2: *Promote and uphold the privacy, dignity, rights, health and wellbeing of people who use health and care services and their carers at all times.*
7. be alert to any changes that could affect a person's needs or progress and report your observations in line with your employer's agreed ways of working.
8. always make sure that your actions or omissions do not harm an individual's health or wellbeing. You must never abuse, neglect, harm or exploit those who use health and care services, their carers or your colleagues.
9. challenge and report dangerous, abusive, discriminatory or exploitative behaviour or practice.
Code of Conduct 3: *Work in collaboration with your colleagues to ensure the delivery of high quality, safe and compassionate healthcare, care and support.* 6. actively encourage the delivery of high quality healthcare, care and support.

[22] **Care Standards**: *17. Good governance.* (1) Systems or processes must be established and operated effectively to ensure compliance with the requirements in this Part. (2) Without limiting paragraph (1), such systems or processes must enable the registered person, in particular, to— (a) assess, monitor and improve the quality and safety of the services provided in the carrying on of the regulated activity (including the quality of the experience of service users in receiving those services); (b) assess, monitor and mitigate the risks relating to the health, safety and welfare of service users and others who may be at risk which arise from the carrying on of the regulated activity; (c) maintain securely an accurate, complete and contemporaneous record in respect of each service user, including a record of the care and treatment provided to the service user and of decisions taken in relation to the care and treatment provided; (d) maintain securely such other records as are necessary to be kept in relation to— (i) persons employed in the carrying on of the regulated activity, and (ii) the management of the regulated activity; (e) seek and act on feedback from relevant persons and other persons on the services provided in the carrying on of the regulated activity, for the purposes of continually evaluating and improving such services; (f) evaluate and improve their practice in respect of the processing of the information referred to in sub-paragraphs (a) to (e). (3) The registered person must send to the Commission, when requested to do so and by no later than 28 days beginning on the day after receipt of the request— (a) a written report setting out how, and the extent to which, in the opinion of the registered person, the requirements of paragraph (2)(a) and (b) are being complied with, and (b) any plans that the registered person has for improving the standard of the

Next is Albert. He needs his night catheter bag emptied. For some reason, the bag is not on a proper catheter bag stand, but in a bin, so André empties the bag into the bin, flushes the urine down the toilet and puts the bag into the bin again without as much as a rinse. Now, this really is going too far. The tall carer understands now the stink of urine in Albert's room during the day. André is very friendly, but this will need to be reported.

The two men go to Mary's room next. The same routine. The way Mary gets pushed about without any warning, you could be looking at a care demonstration carried out with a mannequin. Mary has moved a bit too far down the bed, so she needs to be moved up. Luckily, André is really strong, so he can lift her like a baby and place her on the right spot for the night.

The tall carer has seen enough. So this is what the night shift is like: A show of pushing and rolling puppets. A merry go round of wet pads and bucketfuls of urine. A conference of silence. A pyjama party with rogue hosts and reluctant guests where policy and standard procedure are the biggest jokes.

---

services provided to service users with a view to ensuring their health and welfare.

Pyjama Party

Main point of advice

Institutional abuse and neglect

This story has probably left you with a feeling that you want to have a spare set of eyes to watch over your relative in the care system. Again, institutional abuse. The needs of the institution are put before those of the individual leading to all sorts of neglect. If you have read the previous stories and advice, you must be getting a very good idea of the why and how abuse happens. In this case, a hidden camera would be useful in order to find out what goes on at night. Even without a camera, you can still watch out for clues: smelly carpets, lack of basic equipment such as a catheter stand, untidy rooms, gloves or other personal protection equipment left behind on floors, bags with pads left behind in the bathroom.

Reflection points and positive advice you can offer to carers and managers

1. Is it all right to ask day staff to stay on and help with the night shift?

This is not a good idea as day carers end their shifts feeling tired and not in good physical or mental form to take care of residents on the night shift. Once more we see how management decisions can put vulnerable people at risk. The tall carer has not received the specific training needed for the night shift. He is not aware of night time regulations, and he has not been given the recommended free health assessment for night staff. Also, he hasn't had a chance to go through the recommended period of adaptation. For more information, please visit *GovUK, Employing People*.

2. André seems to break quite a few rules and policies without a care in the world. Why is he not worried about it?

It looks as if André does not realise that he is in the wrong. This could be due to poor training or to lack of proper supervision. In this case, the nurse is present but doesn't say anything, so André's ways seem to represent a *'normal'* night shift in this particular nursing home. The fact that the nurse allows the night shift to carry on in such an unprofessional way has important implications for the tall carer as he feels totally unsupported. It is no wonder that he feels confused and takes so long in reporting the malpractice as he will eventually do.

©Alex Matthews 2018

3. What are your thoughts on the hygiene procedures during the night shift?

Infection control is very deficient on the night shift. Carers carry germs on their gloves as they go from one resident to the next without a change of gloves. Pads get thrown around before being taken out into the corridor, a public area, where there is a bag waiting for them. Urine does not get washed out but it is allowed to sit in buckets overnight in contact with urine bags and catheter tubes.

4. Can you list some of the malpractice in this case study?

In some places such as NHS hospitals, it is all right for two male health professionals to take care of patients, but not in this care home, where they have a policy that forbids it. Hand washing and glove changing recommendations are ignored. Urine sits in buckets in residents' rooms. Moving of residents is done with total disregard for the Moving and Handling policy and regulations. There is no communication with the clients before or during care procedures. There is no supervision of carers' work.

5. Was it all right for the tall carer to just stand and watch all the malpractice?

The tall carer should not have accepted to help with the night shift in the first place. It was wrong of him to let all this malpractice carry on without complaining, but he was probably confused by the nurse's presence. Why didn't she enforce policy and regulations? It was obvious to him that his complaints would fall on deaf ears because the nurse couldn't care less. We have to remember that in a nursing home nurses are line managers. In this particular case, the nurse would have been in charge of the nursing home while the day general manager was off duty until the next morning.

Big Ron's Bed

Now that it's all over, I can laugh about it, I suppose. But it wasn't funny then. I was discharged from hospital in the morning. Not the best time to be dismissed with all the traffic blocking the main roads. By the time we got to the care home, it was after lunch. I say *we* because it was three of us: the driver, the paramedic and me. I would have preferred to go to my own home, but with Jane about to undergo a cancer operation, there was no one to take care of me.

Anyway, it was bad right from the start. When we arrived, they didn't seem to be expecting me at all. I mean, they knew I was coming, but they weren't ready for me. I was asked to wait in a big lounge with the other residents. You should have seen them. They seemed so bored and tired. No one spoke; we just sat there staring at each other. It felt odd. Someone, a nurse presumably, came to tell me that there wasn't a bariatric bed for me but that they would get one soon and that I would be comfortable in one of their single beds[23]. Oh, sorry, *bariatric* is a nice word for huge. In my case, twenty two stones going in all directions, because I'm very tall too. The thing is, I couldn't really move after the operation, so this meant I was bound to a bed that was too small for me.

Transferring me to the tiny bed was a joke. A very unprofessional operation if you ask me. No one knew exactly how to approach the transfer of my bulk from my wheelchair to the bed. Before I knew it, there were four carers and a nurse in my room, all speaking at once, trying to figure out what to do. I might as well not have been there because no one was asking my opinion or preference. If they had asked, I would have told them that I could stand and move, but not for long periods of time. Anyway, they decided to strap me on to a stand aid and sit me on the edge of the bed. And the next step turned out to be another circus performance. No one wanted to help with swinging me into bed. '*I don't want to do my back in*,' they would complain. Or, '*we*

---

[23] **Care Standards**: *17. Good governance*. (1) Systems or processes must be established and operated effectively to ensure compliance with the requirements in this Part. (2) Without limiting paragraph (1), such systems or processes must enable the registered person, in particular, to— (a) assess, monitor and improve the quality and safety of the services provided in the carrying on of the regulated activity (including the quality of the experience of service users in receiving those services); (b) assess, monitor and mitigate the risks relating to the health, safety and welfare of service users and others who may be at risk which arise from the carrying on of the regulated activity; (c) maintain securely an accurate, complete and contemporaneous record in respect of each service user, including a record of the care and treatment provided to the service user and of decisions taken in relation to the care and treatment provided.

have to think about health and safety first.' OK, the nurse and one of the carers left the room. The others got ready to help me swing my legs and back but, when one of the carers tried to raise the bed up so they could do the job safely, the bed would not move. And then they started fussing again as if I wasn't there[24].

'He is too heavy.'

'You must be joking; I'm not risking my back!'

'We'll have to call for help. Maybe the bed is broken,' and so on. As it happened, the bed really was broken[25]. So the next day, they brought another one. Another small bed. But that day he was there, the tall carer, as tall as me only thinner. He was different. At first I thought he was a doctor, or

---

[24] **Care Standards:** *13. Safeguarding service users from abuse and improper treatment.* (1) Service users must be protected from abuse and improper treatment in accordance with this regulation. (2) Systems and processes must be established and operated effectively to prevent abuse of service users. (3) Systems and processes must be established and operated effectively to investigate, immediately upon becoming aware of, any allegation or evidence of such abuse. (4) Care or treatment for service users must not be provided in a way that— (a) includes discrimination against a service user on grounds of any protected characteristic (as defined in section 4 of the Equality Act 2010) of the service user, (b) includes acts intended to control or restrain a service user that are not necessary to prevent, or not a proportionate response to, a risk of harm posed to the service user or another individual if the service user was not subject to control or restraint, (c) is degrading for the service user, or (d) significantly disregards the needs of the service user for care or treatment. (5) A service user must not be deprived of their liberty for the purpose of receiving care or treatment without lawful authority. (6) For the purposes of this regulation— "abuse" means— (a) any behaviour towards a service user that is an offence under the Sexual Offences Act 2003(a), (b) ill-treatment (whether of a physical or psychological nature) of a service user, (c) theft, misuse or misappropriation of money or property belonging to a service user, or (d) neglect of a service user. (7) For the purposes of this regulation, a person controls or restrains a service user if that person— (a) uses, or threatens to use, force to secure the doing of an act which the service user resists, or (b) restricts the service user's liberty of movement, whether or not the service user resists, including by use of physical, mechanical or chemical means.

[25] **Care Standards:** *15. Premises and equipment.* (1) All premises and equipment used by the service provider must be— (a) clean, (b) secure, (c) suitable for the purpose for which they are being used, (d) properly used (e) properly maintained, and (f) appropriately located for the purpose for which they are being used. (2) The registered person must, in relation to such premises and equipment, maintain standards of hygiene appropriate for the purposes for which they are being used. (3) For the purposes of paragraph (1)(b), (c), (e) and (f), "equipment" does not include equipment at the service user's accommodation if— (a) such accommodation is not provided as part of the service user's care or treatment, and (b) such equipment is not supplied by the service provider.

the manager. He looked straight into my eyes and he asked me if I could help them with my moving. He was calm and did not complain about my size. He apologised about all the confusion and the small bed. I liked him straight away. At last someone wanted to know about me. And he was polite and well spoken. I never knew his name. He must have told me his name a few times but, for some reason, it never registered. I called him Mark and Paul and all kinds of different names and he always gave me the same reassuring response: *'That's not my name, Ron, but I like it.'*

What was he doing there? I don't know. What was I doing there? Why did I end up in such a bad home surrounded by amateurs? No bed my size, no manners, nothing to do in my room to pass the time. I would lie there in the most uncomfortable position for hours. My heavy arms falling out of the bed. My feet painfully knocking against the foot board. They must have thought I was mad, the way I cried for help. I always forgot there was a bell to call the carers, so I would yell at the top of my voice. They ended up giving me something to calm down, of course[26]. I know that because the nurses did tell me what they were giving me. And I didn't refuse it.

But it was unbearable. They made an even bigger fuss over me every time. Everything was an issue, from my size, to my weight, to my not very stretchy clothes, to my catheter. Carers could not get me dressed without a lot of effort and complaining. Other times my catheter would bypass for some reason and my whole bed would be soaked in urine. That meant more moving me about to change my clothes and the bed sheets, and more complaining from carers.

The only one who didn't complain was the tall guy. He was always keeping an eye on me. I didn't need to yell when he was about. Always polite and friendly, he would come into my room and offer me a glass of water. But he wasn't always about. Well, maybe he wasn't the only friendly carer, but I just liked him because he didn't make jokes all the time like some of the others. He... How could I put it? He didn't have an attitude. That's it. I do like an attitude, don't get me wrong. But not when you are convalescing and uncomfortable. Everyone who came through the door had an attitude. The joker, or the wincher, or the yeller, or the sexy girl who managed to turn the focus of every conversation into a monologue about her feelings, her life and her body[27]. The tall guy didn't talk about himself and didn't crack jokes.

---

[26] **Care Standards:** *13. Safeguarding service users from abuse and improper treatment.* […] *(7) For the purposes of this regulation, a person controls or restrains a service user if that person— (a) uses, or threatens to use, force to secure the doing of an act which the service user resists, or (b) restricts the service user's liberty of movement, whether or not the service user resists, including by use of physical, mechanical or chemical means.*

[27] **Code of Conduct 2:** *Promote and uphold the privacy, dignity, rights, health and*

Big Ron's Bed

When he was in my room it was all about me and what I needed. Come to think of it, maybe I made him up. Actually, with all the drugs and sleepless nights, he must have been a product of my delirium. Because he didn't fit into that place. And neither did I.

I wanted to leave, but with Jane in hospital it would have been tricky. So I decided to sleep. I would just sleep. What else could I do? But it didn't work out, of course. I slept during the day and spent the nights awake working myself into a frenzy. At night, the home was even worse; it was like being in a different home all together. Those night carers couldn't care less. I could hear them roam around the corridor going into other residents rooms and coming straight out. They would come to my room too, just to check my catheter and pad. No *'hello'*, no words I could understand came out of their mouths. They looked like people from a different world. Sometimes, they would just grin at me like I was crazy or something[28]. I started wondering where I was or if I had already died. That would send me into a panic; I hyperventilated and ran a cold sweat. After a few nights like that, I couldn't eat or drink well and I would just pass out during the day. Once I passed out so that the nurses could not wake me up and decided to send me back to hospital.

Soon I was back in the care home, though. The small bed was waiting for me. And the good news about my wife's successful cancer operation. But that just made me depressed. I would not be able to take care of her. She would not be able to take care of me. I would have to endure the small bed and the awful care for weeks on end. Perhaps for the rest of my days. The future looked so bleak. So I lost it. I went back to yelling for help, to not eating well, to my sleepless nights with the wandering ghosts. They just gave me more drugs to keep me quiet. After a few days of that, I had a massive heart attack.

---

wellbeing of people who use health and care services and their carers at all times. 1. always act in the best interests of people who use health and care services.
2. always treat people with respect and compassion.
3. put the needs, goals and aspirations of people who use health and care services first, helping them to be in control and to choose the healthcare, care and support they receive.
[28] **Care Standards:** *17. Good governance*. (1) Systems or processes must be established and operated effectively to ensure compliance with the requirements in this Part. (2) Without limiting paragraph (1), such systems or processes must enable the registered person, in particular, to— (a) assess, monitor and improve the quality and safety of the services provided in the carrying on of the regulated activity (including the quality of the experience of service users in receiving those services). *Fit and proper persons employed*. (1) Persons employed for the purposes of carrying on a regulated activity must— (a) be of good character.

©Alex Matthews 2018

But I'm OK now. I don't know, maybe if they had given me a bariatric bed in the first place, I wouldn't be dead now. It is all for the best, I suppose. At least, Jane will be able to make a good recovery without having to worry about me all the time. And I hope to God she will never end up in the hands of a rogue care home. Because you'll wish you were dead when that happens.

Main point of advice

Death by neglect
This is a very clear example of institutional abuse happening right from the start. In this case, the abuse leads to an early death. Ron had no-one to watch out for him. His wife was in hospital and I never saw any relatives visiting him. He was one of the most vulnerable members of society and yet, those who had a duty of care towards him failed him completely. If you have read the previous case studies, then you know exactly what advice I am going to give you: never ever let a loved one go to a care home by themselves. If you live abroad (which is very common these days) and cannot accompany your relative through the admission process into a care home, you must get an advocate for them: a family friend, another relative, or a professional. If you can afford it, pay a university student to visit your relative and send you reports on their progress. If Ron had had an advocate when he was admitted to the care home, social services would have been called and they would have forced the care home to move Ron to a bariatric room. As there was no bariatric room in this care home, Ron could have been moved to another care home (the care chain in these stories owns five care homes in the city, so they could easily have done it). With an advocate watching after Ron, he would have got bespoke care rather than the torture he had to endure that led to his early death.

Reflection points and positive advice you can offer to carers and managers

1. Why was Ron not given a bariatric bed?

Not only did the home lack a bariatric bed, but the management didn't realise the importance of giving Ron a bed big enough for him. In this case, the care home management are in breach of several care standards. In particular, *Person-centred care, Safe care and treatment, Safeguarding service users from abuse and improper treatment, Premises and equipment, and Good governance* (Regulations 9, 12, 13, and 17).

2. What are your thoughts on the moving and handling of the client?

In this case, an expert in bariatric care should have been called in order to coordinate all aspects of Ron's care, including the design of a specific moving and handling strategy.

3. Ron concludes that the nursing home was a rogue care home and that the staff who took care of him were amateurs. Is that a fair evaluation?

The care home is probably trying to do the right thing. Surely they are getting a lot of things right and many aspects of the care they offer are excellent. In fact, if they had given Ron a bariatric bed from the start, some of the other negligence and malpractice could have been avoided. This exemplifies just how important it is to get every single aspect of care correct. So, yes, it is a fair evaluation; some aspects of the care given to Ron were rogue and this had disastrous consequences for him.

4. What are the consequences of bad care in this case?

Ron is not given a bariatric bed. This causes extreme discomfort, which is the reason for Ron's crisis. There isn't a specific care plan for Ron that takes into account his size and weight. The moving and handling is done in an utterly amateurish way. Ron does not receive person centred care. The home management seem to be unaware of the potential consequences of the extreme discomfort caused to Ron. Ron spends long hours in his bed with nothing to do. Ron's distress is not taken care of properly. Ron's nutritional needs are neglected.

5. In the previous case study we learn that policy and regulations are not respected on the night shift at this care home. What are some of the consequences for Ron?

The night carers ignore the residents' basic communication needs, they move quickly from one room to the next giving people a fast pad change without asking for consent. Like wandering ghosts, they come in from the dark and speak words that don't make sense to Ron. They certainly contributed to Ron's delusion that he had already died.

6. Do you think Ron imagined the tall carer or is the tall carer a real person? Is it difficult for a carer to display some of the qualities that Ron so appreciated in the tall carer?

In spite of all the neglect, some of Ron's carers must have been good. The tall carer seems to be a product of Ron's imagination. The tall carer helps

Ron keep track in a single person of all the people that come and go, that's why he cannot remember his name. This imaginary person looks like the real tall carer and embodies all the good things done to Ron.

The Party of Endearment

There it is. That light. Soft, gently falling on everything we see, like a mist. The same as that day when we were young. Remember the day the bombing started, Sarah? Are you there, Sarah? Hold my hand. Stay here with me, my love.

Tom is sitting on the sofa. His eyes are closed. Like so many times before, he has gone to a world beyond reason. No one knows exactly where he is, but a few of the carers think that, when he gets into that mood, he goes back to his late wife, Sarah.

German planes, Sarah.
Run to safety.
Hear the bombs.
Embrace me.

But how could he go back to her? His memory is seriously damaged. His capacity for logical thought is severely impaired.

'He has been heard talking to her,' they say. 'He talks to her as if she's really there.'

'But, he cannot speak; he hasn't spoken for ages,' someone retorts.

'He only speaks to her,' another replies.

Why didn't we die then? This is so much worse than German bombs. I can't save you now, Sarah. I can't save myself.

Tom and Harry are holding hands on the sofa. A carer with bright purple hair eggs them on.

'Come on Tom, give him a kiss!'

Her eyes sparkle, her lips throw kisses.

'Oh, they are so sweet!'

Harry now turning towards Tom.

'Go on, Harry. Give him a kiss.'

There is no shame in this. It must be all right to encourage that kind of behaviour. Harry is not really there at all but she won't give up[29].

'Look, Harry, like this.'

She leans forward and embraces Tom, smothering him with slimy kisses and manic laughter. Another carer seems to think that this is fun and sits down next to Harry.

'Hello, love. Give us a kiss. Bu'tiful.'

While the girls encourage the two men to kiss each other, the tall carer in the polo shirt wonders just how far the women are prepared to go.

But Harry is safe. He is not there at all just now. The warm breakfast in his stomach has taken him straight to the tropics, where kind people gather around him.

'Your boat sank.'

'I like it here. Can I stay? You are wonderful. I owe you my life. I'll always keep you in my heart. Thank you for everything you've done. You are wonderful. Thank you. I owe you my life. I like it here. No one died. We are safe. Thank you. Can I stay?'

---

[29] **Care Standards:** *13. Safeguarding service users from abuse and improper treatment.* (1) Service users must be protected from abuse and improper treatment in accordance with this regulation. (2) Systems and processes must be established and operated effectively to prevent abuse of service users. (3) Systems and processes must be established and operated effectively to investigate, immediately upon becoming aware of, any allegation or evidence of such abuse. (4) Care or treatment for service users must not be provided in a way that— (a) includes discrimination against a service user on grounds of any protected characteristic (as defined in section 4 of the Equality Act 2010) of the service user, (b) includes acts intended to control or restrain a service user that are not necessary to prevent, or not a proportionate response to, a risk of harm posed to the service user or another individual if the service user was not subject to control or restraint, (c) is degrading for the service user, or (d) significantly disregards the needs of the service user for care or treatment. (5) A service user must not be deprived of their liberty for the purpose of receiving care or treatment without lawful authority. (6) For the purposes of this regulation— "abuse" means— (a) any behaviour towards a service user that is an offence under the Sexual Offences Act 2003(a), (b) ill-treatment (whether of a physical or psychological nature) of a service user, (c) theft, misuse or misappropriation of money or property belonging to a service user, or (d) neglect of a service user.

©Alex Matthews 2018

The Party of Endearment

Almost everyone has congregated in the lounge. Breakfast is over. The morning rush is forgotten. Some carers are completing care plans. There is music playing and cheerleaders laughing at the two lover boys. Most residents are sitting comfortably, waiting for their cup of tea.

Malcolm starts his clucking and all heads turn to him. Now the cheerleaders become mocking birds. *Cluck, cluck, cluck*, some repeat after Malcolm[30].

'Isn't he lovely?' they say, fussing all around him. *'He looks like a teddy bear.'*

Malcolm wants to speak. But his words have become a cluck and a coo and, when he speaks, he can hear mocking echoes.

'Cluck, cluck, cluck, Malcolm. Want a kiss, love? A dirty old man, he is. He'll put his hands all over you if you're not careful.'

But Malcolm can't see well. His eyes are covered in ointment. He looks as if he has been crying. Perhaps he has. His hands reach out in an effort to grab somebody. He needs to say something.

Cluck, cluck, cluck.

Somebody listen, please. I need my glasses. Where are my glasses. But no one understands his clucking and now he is trying to stand up.

'Sit down, Malcolm! You'll fall over.'

'Cluck, cluck, cluck.'

Everyone laughs. Well, not everyone. The tall carer in the polo shirt is not amused at all, even if everything is done in a festive mood intended to liven up the party.

'Malcolm, your wife will be here soon. You'll be alright then.'

---

[30]**Code of Conduct 2:** *Promote and uphold the privacy, dignity, rights, health and wellbeing of people who use health and care services and their carers at all times.* 1. always act in the best interests of people who use health and care services. 2. always treat people with respect and compassion. 3. put the needs, goals and aspirations of people who use health and care services first, helping them to be in control and to choose the healthcare, care and support they receive.[…] 8. always make sure that your actions or omissions do not harm an individual's health or wellbeing. You must never abuse, neglect, harm or exploit those who use health and care services, their carers or your colleagues. 9. challenge and report dangerous, abusive, discriminatory or exploitative behaviour or practice.

©Alex Matthews 2018

But Malcolm is scared of his wife's visits. He needs her so much, but when she is actually here, there is only recrimination. *Why do you keep me here? I can't see, I can't walk, I can't speak. And you leave me here alone. I want to be home. Oh, how I wish I could control my anger. I so badly want to be home with you. Everyone just laughs at me here. I want to be home. I want to be home. I want to be home. I want to be home.*

'Look, his eyes are quite red and watery now. We'll have to call the nurse.'

'He'll be alright. It's the ointment. Want a cuddle? That's what you want. Isn't it? Here. Look at your face. How ungrateful! Give us a smile, Malcolm[31].'

And the chorus of mocking birds bursts into laughter again. *Coo, coo, coo.* And there is no tropical island where Malcolm can hide, no guardian angel to hold his hand.

---

[31] **Code of Conduct 3:** *Work in collaboration with your colleagues to ensure the delivery of high quality, safe and compassionate healthcare, care and support*: […]
5. honour your work commitments, agreements and arrangements and be reliable, dependable and trustworthy.
6. actively encourage the delivery of high quality healthcare, care and support.

©Alex Matthews 2018

The Party of Endearment

Main point of advice

Sexual abuse
It is surprising how few people understand that unwanted affection constitutes sexual abuse. I recently spent a few weeks as a senior team leader in a top-end care home where I discovered a case of sexual abuse: a male carer kissing a ninety-year-old dementia sufferer on the lips with his body all over the lady. When I disclosed this to the manager and the other care leaders, they all told me that I didn't understand the type of dementia care that was being applied at the care home. We had four meetings about the same topic and each time they said that giving physical affection to the residents was an essential part of their approach. What they don't understand at this care home is that unwanted affection is abuse. A person with dementia can seem to welcome kisses and hugs, but how can we really know that they are making an informed choice? Besides, if you examine carefully who gets hugs and kisses in a care home, you will find that it is always the same *sweet* and *lovely* residents who get them. The rest don't get the same attention. This discriminatory treatment is in itself objectionable. On the other hand, the management of the home have a duty to protect its carers from getting into trouble with the law. If an inspector had turned up unannounced and seen the abuse, or if someone had happened to take a photo, the carer would have ended up in court.

As regards the lewd behaviour of the carers in this case study, it is a direct result of poor management. When you visit your relative at the care home you have to be watchful of the carers: are they using terms of endearment? This is not professional. Are they physically affectionate? This could be a sign of lax safeguarding. If they know that you don't approve, they will treat your relative with dignity and respect.

Reflection points and positive advice you can offer to carers and managers

1. How does the carers' humiliating behaviour affect the ethos of the care business?

This kind of behaviour turns the whole business into a mockery where other aspects of care could also suffer. It creates a culture of informality and humiliation that has a very negative impact on the residents.

©Alex Matthews 2018

2. What are your thoughts on the hiring, training and supervision of staff in this case?

It looks as if there are some deficiencies in the hiring process at the care home. The fundamental standards state clearly in Section 19, *Fit and proper persons employed*, paragraph (1), that it is the responsibility of the registered manager to hire *'persons of good character'*. Also, under the same section, paragraph (2), *'Recruitment procedures must be established and operated effectively to ensure that persons employed meet the conditions in [...] paragraph (1)'*. As regards training, not enough emphasis has been placed on teaching carers how to safeguard service users from abuse and improper treatment. Finally, it is obvious that supervision instruments have been sabotaged. In this case study we find all residents and carers in the lounge. Presumably, one or two of the carers must have been care coordinators, and it is likely that a nurse was also coming in and out of the room, and yet nobody complained about the carers' lewd and mocking behaviour. All this points to serious mismanagement of the nursing home, which contravenes the regulations laid out by the Care Act in *Requirements relating to registered managers* where it is stated that '*a person is not fit to be a registered manager in respect of a regulated activity unless the said person has the necessary qualifications, skills and experience to manage the carrying on of the regulated activity*' (*The Health and Social Care Act 2008 (Regulated Activities) Regulations, Part 3*. Based on the unchecked abuse that we can see in these case studies, the skills and experience of the manager would need to be questioned.

3. What is allowing this kind of mockery to go on?

This question has been partly answered in 2 above. The care home has not implemented a strong supervisory strategy which means that some of the carers seem to run the place to the detriment of the clients.

4. What care standards are being broken in this case study and why?

Out of the twelve fundamental standards in the Care Act, at least seven have been broken in this case study: *Person-centred care, Dignity and respect, Need for consent, Safeguarding service users from abuse and improper treatment, Good governance, Staffing,* and *Fit and proper persons employed* (Regulations 9, 10, 11, 13, 17, 18 and 19).

5. The tall carer is not amused by the mockery and humiliation being inflicted on the residents, but he is not doing anything to stop it. Why?

The Party of Endearment

The tall carer realises that this kind of behaviour is fairly common at the dementia unit as it is done in public and is approved by all the other carers, including senior staff and line managers, so he doesn't see the point in complaining about it.

6. How is Malcolm's groping being misunderstood? How is he being stereotyped?

Malcolm just needs to find his glasses. His groping for his glasses is misunderstood for improper sexual behaviour. Malcolm is both being neglected and stereotyped as a dirty old man, which clearly violates the standards in *Person centred care* and in *Dignity and respect* (Regulations 9 and 10).

Ten Minutes

Nicola needs her mum to die. All the grieving was done a long time ago when mum first stopped recognising her own daughter. Then mum went into a minimally conscious state and has remained like that for six years. Fortunately, the home has phoned to say that mum has taken a turn for the worse. Pneumonia, apparently. And just like every time mum has been poorly before, the doctor is instructed to provide palliative medication only. Perhaps this time she will really die. But that's what you get when you put your loved ones in a high-end care home: they don't die fast enough.

Jackie is one of only four spouses who come to the home daily to spend time with their loved ones. Even if their loved ones can no longer recognise them, talk to them or even embrace them. *Till death do us part*, a vow spoken so briefly such a long time ago, is now a most meaningful daily reality for these faithful few.

Jackie comes to the home and helps with a lot with her husband's care. Like so many of her generation, she will not be heard complaining that she is tired or ill. If the weather is awful, she will still be there on time, shaking a soaked umbrella. When she is not well enough to drive her car, she will make it to the home by bus. And the same can be said for the other two wives and the husband who faithfully come to the home every day to fulfil that old promise. But, of course, they understand something that a lot of people cannot see or even imagine.

Six years having a mother and not having a mother at the same time is more than anyone can bear. So Nicola only comes to the home when mum is poorly and there is a chance that she might die. On those few days that she comes to the home, she talks to the nurses, brings in a doctor, then she gets on the phone, and she might even give her mother a drink. But, once again, Nicola's mum pulls through. Nicky is clearly upset and can be seen walking frantically around the home, talking to the doctor and the nurses, lifting her arms in the air, nodding her head not being able to understand the irony of it, of life not wanting to expire yet. Better luck next time.

Paul often comes to the home to visit his dad, Tom. He always seems quite excited to see dad, but the excitement wears off as soon as he realises that, as usual, dad does not respond to his warm greetings. Dad does not even seem to recognise him. Soon, Paul has had enough and is saying his good byes. It is always the same, Paul. Don't fool yourself: dad really is gone; he does not know who you are. For Paul it's a long dark good bye.

Tom gets to spend a lot of time with one-to-one carers. Not for ten minutes at a time. They usually spend eight-hour shifts with him. Even fourteen-hour shifts sometimes. And these carers know that Tom can recognise people. He may not know his carers by name and he may not even be able to tell them apart, but he knows that they are his carers.

The tall carer has been with Tom a lot. And he is getting used to Tom's dark moments. Tom can get quite aggressive, fighting and shouting, trying to get away from carers, throwing things around. He will then run out of energy and sit or lie down with his eyes closed for a while. When he eventually comes to, his eyes will be met by his carer's eyes. Tom will then smile and exclaim *'Oh, good! Where were we?'* Other times, he will be full of grateful words; he will hold his carer's hand and call him his son. These moments are cherished by the tall carer, and they would be cherished by Paul if he were able to spend more than ten minutes with his dad when he comes to visit.

And that is precisely the spouses' secret: their loved ones are gone... Until they are back. Because they do visit occasionally. They get back from the darkness of dementia just for a fleeting moment, they look at you in the eye, they might say something, and then they are gone again. But you have to be there if you want to catch that moment. And the tall carer is not going to tell Nicola that her mum sometimes looks at him in the eye and, faintly smiling, squeezes his hand with affection. This stubborn woman is not interested in dying. She may not recognise people anymore. She may not know who she is. But something inside her wants her to live on even if the people around her think it is high time she died.

Main point of advice

Advocacy

If you have read the previous chapters, then you'll have realised by now that advocacy is the most effective weapon in the fight against abuse. Perhaps the reassurance that someone is taking care of your relative, thinking that they are in good hands and you don't need to worry, is precisely where abuse begins to germinate. 'She'll be alright.' That's what a lot of people think. But how can an abandoned parent ever be all right? They are not. We need to be there, with them. That's the first step. But being there alone is not enough. We also have to keep our eyes open and always demand a high quality of care. The husband and wives mentioned in the story that came to visit almost every day really believed that their spouses were in good hands, but they weren't. They all suffered from rough handling and neglect. In the whole care home, I only witnessed two cases of relatives who actively demanded good quality of care and their loved ones did get quality of care. There was also a respite resident who had her whole family practically living in the care home with her: husband, sons, daughters, and grandchildren. They turned up in the morning, and took turns to spend the whole day there, interacting with the residents and the carers, and they left in the evening. The husband was at the care home all day long. The sons and daughters came often. The grandchildren would arrive after school. It was lovely to see it. Perhaps this reflection puts the onus of preventing abuse on the relatives rather than the care system. But what happens with those who have no relatives to come and visit them? Even those with no visits benefit from the company and friendship of people who come to the care home, not only because of their company, but because visitors actually lessen the burden on the carers every time they take care of their own relatives, every time they keep somebody else company, every time they pass on a message to the carers.

Reflection points and positive advice you can offer to carers and managers

1. When a client lacks mental capacity, someone else will be making decisions for them. In this case study it is the daughter and a doctor who decide to stop medication and let mother die.

A few days after Nicola's mum had died, the tall carer was invited to a training session on end of life care. The session was organised by the

County Council and the NHS. During this training session, the tall carer learned that a lot of people who lack mental capacity are allowed to die if they stop eating or drinking. Doctors and relatives conclude that the person *'wants'* to die, so they decide to let the person die a *'natural and dignified'* death. But the person could be suffering from nausea or a number of other treatable conditions. Is it all right to let people die just because they can't communicate, because they are old, because they have dementia?

2. How can we be sure that someone in the advanced stages of dementia is ready to die?

It is impossible to know what goes on inside the mind of a dementia sufferer. A care manager should respect and guard their clients' right to life. If a young person develops an eating disorder and they cannot eat or drink, they are given all the necessary medical help they need, regardless of whether they possess mental capacity or not. It should be the same when our clients are old and vulnerable.

3. A natural death?

Care workers come across people who are in a hurry for their relatives to die. There are also managers and doctors who are too eager to please these relatives by withdrawing medication so the client dies a *'natural death'*. But what is a natural death? Is letting someone starve till they die a natural death? You will need to make sure that your relative is really beyond medical help before allowing the care home to stop all food and fluids. Perhaps you could seek a second medical opinion before letting your relative die from dehydration and malnutrition in their care home bed.

4. The tall carer does not interfere in the relationships between the clients and their relatives. He could tell the relatives to spend more time with their loved ones so they can find that special moment when a connection is made. But he doesn't. Why?

The tall carer doesn't interfere with the relationship between the clients and their relatives for a number of reasons. First of all, telling people how they should treat their relatives is beyond a carer's role. On the other hand, offering advice with relationships of any kind is probably not a good idea unless you are a counsellor or a psychologist. Besides, the tall carer's observations are subjective. When a person is in the advanced stages of dementia, there is no way of knowing why they smile at you or why they are happy to see you. In fact, there is no way of knowing what they are really seeing. And there is certainly no way of knowing if they are back or not from dementia for a fleeting moment. The tall carer decides to believe that they are really back sometimes and that the moment of happiness is worth it, but this is just his impression; so it is correct of him not to tell anyone about it.

5. What do you think is the effect of having regular visitors? Think about the effect on all the residents and the general atmosphere of the nursing home.

When a care home receives the general public, a community atmosphere is created. The more visitors, including volunteers, relatives and services providers, the more lively and pleasant it is for everyone, including care workers. So, in this case, the faithful spouses' role goes beyond that of paying a visit to their relative. There are care homes that run coffee shops and other services open to the general public. This helps avoid the isolation that their residents might otherwise feel.

Hitler Is Alive

'Hitler will kill us all,' shouts a loud manly voice. *'We are all dead! The world is ending!'*

Daphne has been removed from the dining room again. Her loud screams upset everyone – the other residents, the visitors, the nurse, the waitress and the carers. She is now sitting in her room remembering the concentration camp, and warning the world about our near end. She has gone to that private dark place. And in this dark place Daphne talks to her dead relatives as if they were there with her. Mary, her across-the-corridor neighbour knows them all by name. Mary was a victim of Nazi Germany too. Her dad was killed in one of the first surprise bombings in England at the beginning of the war. Her mother, a nurse, had to stop working in order to take care of their four children. Mary's mother refused having her children sent to safe areas in the country. She wanted to keep what was left of the family together. So Mary knows quite a bit about bombs and fear, and she loves Daphne in spite of her screaming.

Few of the people who saw action on the front are still here with us. Most of our residents were too young to fight. But they were not too young to be bombed. And they were not too young to be locked away in concentration camps. At the end of the war, Daphne was liberated and taken to the UK as a war refugee. She grew up as a British citizen, married, had children. She was given a new life in a new country. She even forgot her mother tongue as well as the events that turned her into an orphan. But, in her old age, schizophrenia sends her back to the camp, and now she is there most of the time waiting for her relatives to be taken one by one to the gas chambers. The only liberation for her now will be death.

Frank is a volunteer who comes from time to time to keep the residents company. He is not young himself so he can remember the war. And he brings up that topic of conversation sometimes. Then you see people paying attention. They gather around him as if he were some kind of shaman. A medicine man who can bring memory back to those who lost it. People who no longer watch television, no longer pay any attention to newspapers or to music are now listening carefully. A lot of them remember the bomb shelters, the food rationing, the separation of families, the lost fortunes, and the bad news about dead or wounded family members. Those who can walk get closer. A circle is formed.

'The bomb shelter in the garden. Do you remember that?' enquires the shaman.

'Gathering around the kitchen radio waiting for news. Remember that?'

'Yes. We had a bomb shelter in the garden. A family lived in it.'

Those who can talk contribute with their memories. Real or made up on the spot, are fitting for the occasion. Reminiscence therapy, they call it. Frank is good at it. It all seems real. It is all in the present. Hitler is alive. And so is the spirit that defeated him.

But you wouldn't think the residents here brave enough to fight Hitler, judging by the way some of them whine. Mike spends the whole day screaming *'help me, help me'* at the top of his voice. He does this with the even cry and conformist feeling of a wheelbarrow-pushing fishmonger. Sometimes he throws in existential questions for free, *'I've had enough. I can't stand it anymore! What have I done to deserve this? Did I kill anyone?'* Other times he goes minimalistic: *'help, help'*. Only the final letter gets dropped, so what you hear is *'hell, hell, hell'* for hours on end. Or maybe he does mean to say *hell*.

We have more than one war refugee at the home. Ruth has been here for ten years. She was in the early stages of dementia when she first came and, according to some carers who knew her then, she used to sing and play piano. She is bed bound now. She hardly ever opens her eyes, but she can still swallow and special care is given to serve her kosher meals. Ruth looks like an angel. She has this permanent smile on her lips as if saying *'thank you'*. Or maybe she has understood a fundamental truth and is now at peace with what happened to her: losing her family and being raised by adoptive parents in postwar hardship; the effort she made to put the horror of persecution and extermination behind; the torture of becoming something else; the crippling guilt of having escaped and survived; the guilty pleasure of love and having her own family; and then losing everything to dementia and being dumped in a care home where she gets no visits from friends or family. What happened to the people in her life? Is dementia scarier than Hitler?

But most residents in the dementia unit do not have angelic smiles on their faces. Most are not enjoying the peaceful autumn of their lives. There are *the runners,* for example. They run around the unit like haunted souls. They bang on walls and doors. '*I want to go home*, they scream. *Take me home!*'

Jean is an elegant tall woman. She had been a school teacher. She suffered a massive stroke eight years ago. One day she was a retired teacher, next day she had full blown dementia-like symptoms and couldn't remember who she was. Jean packs her bag every evening and walks to the door of the dementia unit. '*I'm going to London*, she says, *I'm catching the next train.*' But the residents in the dementia unit have lost a very important human right, the right of free movement. They are kept behind locked doors for their own protection. Jean could spend the next eight years packing her bags, living the same day over and over again. Her dementia is not expected to get worse, so she is living Groundhog Day, trapped in the same day for ever.

'Hitler will kill us all,' shouts Daphne from her room. Her neighbour, Mary, is not a dementia sufferer. No one really knows why she is here in the dementia unit. Mary, a retired nurse, likes to comfort Daphne in her own particular way.

'Don't worry, Daphne, your brothers are here with me playing. I'm taking care of them. You can go back to sleep now.'

But Daphne is not really here at the moment, so she cannot hear Mary and she will keep screaming for a while. *'They are coming to get us! We are all dead! The World is ending!'*

However, Daphne is not the only screamer, or even the loudest. Jack spends every day in his room shouting *'kill me, kill me'* in a husky smoker's voice. He is one of the few residents who fought at the front. He was a very young Royal Air Force pilot and he only flew strategic raids over Germany at the very end of the war. Jack knows a lot about rage. It is impossible to know what causes his rage, but a lot of people must have felt just like him after the Blitz. Jack spends the whole day in a foul mood. He shouts the vilest insults at carers, throws punches and spits at them. He also throws crockery and glasses against the walls, so his meals are served on plastic plates.

'Kill me!'

Riley is a young carer who has been working at the home for over a year and knows the ropes. He does not like to do one-to-one care work though, and he has been heard saying the f-word when talking about spending one-to-one time with Tom. *'I've been f*king stuck in a room for six f*king hours!'*[32] Tom is one of the runners. He bangs on walls, he tries to get out, he fights and bites. But he can also spend hours sitting in his room, gone. And it is boring to sit there for ages waiting for him to wake up and bite you. But Tom is not sitting down now. He has been walking around, going into other residents' rooms, knocking things over, spilling drinks, and giving his carer plenty of reason to swear.

---

[32]**Care Standards:** *19. Fit and proper persons employed.* (1) Persons employed for the purposes of carrying on a regulated activity must— (a) be of good character, (b) have the qualifications, competence, skills and experience which are necessary for the work to be performed by them, and (c) be able by reason of their health, after reasonable adjustments are made, of properly performing tasks which are intrinsic to the work for which they are employed.

The young carer is trying to convince Tom to sit down in the lounge, but Tom has other plans. He sits down for a minute and then stands up. The young carer is becoming a bit forceful now and some of the other staff members are getting concerned. Not all of them though. The young carer is a popular boy and has a pair of female cronies who listen to him and laugh at his jokes. Now the cronies dance around Tom laughing. Still, no one says anything critical, as usual. Tom tries to dash for the exit and the young carer has had enough. With the skill of a prison guard, he pushes a wheelchair against the back of Tom's knees while one of the girls forces Tom to fall into it. The young carer fastens the safety belt and Tom is safely captured[33].

'Are we allowed to restrain people like that?'

'No, we are not. I don't know what they are doing.'

The other carers in the lounge are puzzled by the events, but they decide to wait and see what happens. Perhaps there is a good reason to restrain Tom. The young carers disappear into the kitchen for a cup of tea and a chat while Tom desperately tries to stand up. *'He'll be alright'* they say as they turn their backs on him. Tom's energy level is at a low ebb at the moment, so he is moving his arms and legs like an upside-down insect unable to flip itself over.

'Hitler will kill us all!'

'Kill me! Kill me, please!'

'I'm going to London. Let me out.'

'Your brothers are here with me. They are safe.'

---

[33] **Care Standards:** *13. Safeguarding service users from abuse and improper treatment.* (1) Service users must be protected from abuse and improper treatment in accordance with this regulation. (2) Systems and processes must be established and operated effectively to prevent abuse of service users. (3) Systems and processes must be established and operated effectively to investigate, immediately upon becoming aware of, any allegation or evidence of such abuse. (4) Care or treatment for service users must not be provided in a way that— (a) includes discrimination against a service user on grounds of any protected characteristic (as defined in section 4 of the Equality Act 2010) of the service user, (b) includes acts intended to control or restrain a service user that are not necessary to prevent, or not a proportionate response to, a risk of harm posed to the service user or another individual if the service user was not subject to control or restraint, (c) is degrading for the service user, or (d) significantly disregards the needs of the service user for care or treatment. (5) A service user must not be deprived of their liberty for the purpose of receiving care or treatment without lawful authority.

©Alex Matthews 2018

'Kill me!'

'The world is ending!'

'No, thank you. I don't want any tea. I'm off to London. Let me out, please.'

'He'll be alright.'

'Hell, hell!'

The tall carer cannot shut them up. The voices are there in his head all the time. He can hear them when he is in his own home. Sometimes, he wakes up in the middle of the night and they are there, screaming, in lonely beds, or banging on doors trying to escape. Their nightmare dementia is becoming his dementia nightmare.

Daphne is taken away just like she predicted. She wasn't wrong about that. She spends the day vomiting and carers discover unexplained bruises all over her body. So they come and take her away. Two days later, the home is informed of her passing.

Jack is also gone, because people are taken away and they die before you can even finish writing about them. Eventually, everyone in the concentration camp will die, even Mary with her white lies, and Ruth, with her beautiful smile, Mike, with his cockle wheelbarrow, and Tom. Death will set them free.

Hitler Is Alive

Main point of advice

Physical abuse
In this story, a resident is restrained in plain view of the other residents and carers. Also, another resident is taken to hospital after being found covered in 'unexplained' bruises. If your relative is living in a dementia unit, you have to be mentally prepared for all the unpleasantness that you will see while you are there visiting. Any abuse you witness needs to be reported to the manager. They will not do anything about it, but it will guarantee better treatment for your relative. This book is giving you the tools to see exactly what constitutes abuse and on what grounds you could report it. When the management at care home realise that you are in the know, they will be careful at least with your own relative.

Reflection points and positive advice you can offer to carers and managers

1. This is not the only case study where we find a resident who does not suffer from dementia locked up in a dementia unit. Can you think of any good reasons why someone, or their relatives, would choose to live in a dementia unit?

The dementia unit where the tall carer worked did admit residents who did not live with the condition. The relatives gave different reasons for this. Some liked the lively atmosphere. There are more carers in a dementia unit because some challenging residents receive one-to-one care. Others thought it would be safer for their relatives to be in a locked up ward. While locking people up in a dementia unit might be illegal because it infringes their basic human rights, the fact is that there is extreme suffering and unpleasantness going on all the time in such a place. A dementia unit is not appropriate for anybody who is not a dementia sufferer or their carer.

2. Why did young Riley restrain Tom? Could it have been avoided?

Riley restrained Tom because the young man was frustrated and bored. Riley had let everyone know that he didn't like to do one-to-one work. Had the management of the home been more receptive to Riley's preferences, this situation could have been avoided. Also, it seems as if Riley hadn't been reminded about the restraining policy before coming into contact with a challenging resident.

3. The tall carer can no longer take the strain of working in a dementia unit. Can anyone work in a dementia unit? Should there be psychometric tests (i.e. psychological and aptitudinal assessments) before letting new carers join a dementia care team?

Obviously, dementia care is not for everyone. Psychological, aptitudinal and vocational tests could be offered to people who want to pursue a career in dementia care. This would be in line with the standards in *Staffing* and also in *Fit and proper persons employed* (Regulations 18 and 19).

4. What Codes of Conduct did Riley break?

Riley broke codes 1, 2 and 3. Please refer to Appendix 2.

5. The tall carer is getting drawn into the residents' dementia in a dangerous way.

The tall carer was very motivated to work in dementia care, but he wasn't aware of his own limitations. Perhaps the only way to know where your limits are when it comes to something like dementia care is to give it a try.

The tall carer would have benefited from a support group where he could have discussed all the issues that he was encountering during his day-to-day work. This could have been organised by the nursing home management.

Set 4

If you end up in set four for whatever reason, you'll be scarred for life. You would have to be lucky to move up and out of that losers club, and to be invited into the more elite sets two and set one[34]. But those are the idiosyncrasies of the British education system. Anyway, somebody has to work in a care home; you can't always hire foreign engineers and foreign teachers to wipe bottoms.

The tall carer was an English teacher before he decided to change careers and start from scratch. And he has come to realise that a lot of the carers at the home cannot construct a full sentence or spell very well. The evidence is all in the progress logs. Carers are required to faithfully document the help that they have given and the ex-teacher had a strange urge to cry the first time he read through some of his colleagues' two-word entries. He knew then that he was working with set-four material. When he read those weak sentences, the cruelty of it hit him: *these adults cannot write*…

Norma is a lonely woman. She is hated by everyone in the home. She is so lonely that she spends the whole day ringing her bell for attention, calling the carers every five minutes, and that rubs Donna up the wrong way.

'What do you want now Norma? Don't you realise we are busy?'

'I just wanted to know what's for tea.'

'A lot of people want to know what's for tea, Norma. I want to know many things. But I have to wait. Just like everybody else.'

'I know… I just…'

'Norma, if you ring that bell again, I don't know what's gonna happen! Let us do our work and just wait till tea time. Then you'll know what's for tea. Seriously, some people!'

But set four is not just about academic failure. It is all about territoriality and bullying; gossip and humiliation; rebellion and sabotage. And that behaviour of failure has all cascaded down to the care home. '*I can't believe the fibs in this place. It's like being back in high school,*' complains one of the new carers. Obviously, when he started, he did not know that most new carers

---

[34] In many British schools, students are streamed into "sets". More able and well behaved students go to sets one and two, and set four is reserved for the least academically able students as well as for disruptive students.

©Alex Matthews 2018

are greeted with gossip and hostility. You see them motivated, animated and smiling during their first week, only to watch the smiles wear off and give way to perpetual frowning after a few days. But, when they work you to the bone, you don't want newbies coming along with smiles and enthusiasm, you want to work with experienced carers like yourself. People who have got time management down to a fine art. People who can do the job and will make your shift more bearable[35].

Set four systematically undermines processes without even thinking about it. At school they subvert the order of learning and now they subvert the crucial functionality of a system under strain. It is learnt behaviour that's ingrained so badly it starts to look more like inborn behaviour, so the line managers (like the teachers) do not have an easy time. Set four knows how to handle authority all right and Donna is very good at putting nurses in their place.

'I hope you don't mind me saying it, but certain people don't like helping. And they are the ones causing the trouble, not me.'

'OK, Donna. Would you mind giving me a list of names privately?'

'Yes, I can do that.'

But the people on that list will be whistle blowers themselves, pointing the finger at each other, and the nurses will be going round in circles, wasting their time, taken for a ride by set four. Or even worse, direct orders and guidelines given and agreed by everyone during staff meetings and handovers will be followed by a secret meeting of subversion, where you will hear carers stealthily decide that the people in management don't have a lot of common sense. Meaning, of course, that the orders will not be followed by any of the carers.

A sixteen-year-old girl has started working at the home. She has only been there for a few weeks, but she is quickly learning to adopt the stern attitude and tone of voice of the prison officer. She is now in Norma's room. Personal

---

[35] **Care Standards:** *19. Fit and proper persons employed.* (1) Persons employed for the purposes of carrying on a regulated activity must— (a) be of good character, (b) have the qualifications, competence, skills and experience which are necessary for the work to be performed by them, and (c) be able by reason of their health, after reasonable adjustments are made, of properly performing tasks which are intrinsic to the work for which they are employed. (2) Recruitment procedures must be established and operated effectively to ensure that persons employed meet the conditions in— (a) paragraph (1), or (b) in a case to which regulation 5 applies, paragraph (3) of that regulation. (3) The following information must be available in relation to each such person employed— (a) the information specified in Schedule 3, and (b) such other information as is required under any enactment to be kept by the registered person in relation to such persons employed.

Set 4

and continence care has been provided by the young girl and another carer. Now they are just tidying up before going to the next resident.

'Do you want your curtains open, Norma?' she asks.

'Can I have my TV on, please?' replies Norma.

'Do you want your curtains open?'

'I'd like my TV on, please.'

'Do you want your curtains open or not?'

'Of course you can have your TV on,' interrupts the tall carer. *'Anything else we can do for you?'*

'No. Thank you. I just wanted my TV on.'

Norma is causing so much disruption that a nurse is called in to help with the situation. So next time Norma's bell rings, there is a little lecture ready for her in a stern tone of voice.

'I need my pad checked.'

'Norma, you've just had a pad change. We are very busy. Everyone here needs care. We cannot spend the whole time with you. You are not the only one. We don't have one-to-one care here in the residential unit. Unless you want to move to the dementia unit. There are more carers there to answer your calls. Otherwise, you need to stop ringing your bell.'

'No. I don't want to move. Thank you[36].'

---

[36] **Care Standards**: 9. *Person-centred care*. (1) The care and treatment of service users must— (a) be appropriate, (b) meet their needs, and (c) reflect their preferences. (2) But paragraph (1) does not apply to the extent that the provision of care or treatment would result in a breach of regulation 11. (3) Without limiting paragraph (1), the things which a registered person must do to comply with that paragraph include— (a) carrying out, collaboratively with the relevant person, an assessment of the needs and preferences for care and treatment of the service user; (b) designing care or treatment with a view to achieving service users' preferences and ensuring their needs are met; (c) enabling and supporting relevant persons to understand the care or treatment choices available to the service user and to discuss, with a competent health care professional or other competent person, the balance of risks and benefits involved in any particular course of treatment; (d) enabling and supporting relevant persons to make, or participate in making, decisions relating to the service user's care or treatment to the maximum extent possible; (e) providing opportunities for relevant persons to manage the

A few minutes later, Norma rings again, of course. This time it is the tall carer who comes to see what she wants. When Norma sees the friendly carer, she greets him with a cheeky smile.

'Hello, Norma. What can I do for you?'

'Will the night staff check my pad?'

'Of course they will, Norma. But we still have three hours to go before the night shift. We will check your pad before that.'

'Can you check it now.'

'Sure. Let me close the door.'

The tall carer knows he cannot afford the time; there are quite a few residents waiting for personal care. Besides, the home leadership are coming down hard on poor time management.

'It's a bit wet, but not too much. We'll come and change it for you in a few minutes.'

'OK, but don't forget, will you.'

'No, Norma. And please try not to ring the bell so much. It's only two of us for this corridor, and everyone needs care.'

Norma responds well to patience and smiles. Who doesn't? So her bell will be quiet for a little while. But even in a private high-end care home you can end up in set four and Norma is learning the rules of rebellion and sabotage. So she will not let her carers do their jobs in peace. She will cause an interruption every five minutes; just like a set-four student.

---

service user's care or treatment; (f) involving relevant persons in decisions relating to the way in which the regulated activity is carried on in so far as it relates to the service user's care or treatment; (g) providing relevant persons with the information they would reasonably need for the purposes of sub-paragraphs (c) to (f); (h) making reasonable adjustments to enable the service user to receive their care or treatment; (i) where meeting a service user's nutritional and hydration needs, having regard to the service user's well-being. (4) Paragraphs (1) and (3) apply subject to paragraphs (5) and (6). (5) If the service user is 16 or over and lacks capacity in relation to a matter to which this regulation applies, paragraphs (1) to (3) are subject to any duty on the registered person under the 2005 Act in relation to that matter. (6) But if Part 4 or 4A of the 1983 Act applies to a service user, care and treatment must be provided in accordance with the provisions of that Act.

©Alex Matthews 2018

Jameela was hired as a care coordinator a year ago. She has Health and Social Care certificates and she is also doing a degree in Social Care. But she hasn't received training on how to handle sabotage, so she has already given up on trying to do the right thing.

'I don't care anymore. When I started here, I tried to change many things, but no one was interested. The carers here think they run the place and they don't want changes. They hated me. They opposed every single improvement I suggested. So I don't care anymore. I just try to do my job the best I can and go home and forget about it.'

'I know what you mean, Jamee. You can't change their ways.'

'They work without gloves. They throw pads on the floor. There is no infection control.'

'It's a lot worse in the dementia unit though. Over there, carers fling dirty pads on tables and chairs; you see faces covered in dribble, medicine spilled on the floors. There is something very wrong in this place.'

'Yeah, tell me about it. I'm so fed up. I came here thinking I was making a good career move, thinking this was a five-star care home.'

'We'll be lucky if we don't get closed down for good.'

'If this care home wasn't so close to my house, I'd consider getting another job.'

'It wouldn't be a bad idea to get out before the boat sinks.'

'It isn't worth it; you'll find the same problems and worse wherever you go. I'd go back to teaching if I were you.'

It is good to vent one's frustrations with the care coordinator, but Norma's bell is ringing again. The tall carer knows that this time she will really need a pad change, so he goes and finds his partner, Donna.

'She'll have to wait! I'm not going to Norma. She's down right rude that woman. She needs to learn some respect.'

'I'll change her pad if you don't mind.'

'You do what you like. But don't take too long, we need to crack on.'

'OK, Donna. I'll find you as soon as I'm finished.'

Set 4

But this is set four and it is all about revenge and humiliation. So Norma is waiting in a stinking paddle of urine and runny faeces that flow freely out of her pad.

'Oh, dear... Norma! I can't change your pad by myself. This is too much. I'll have to get help.'

'I told you I needed a pad change.'

'OK. Please wait for one more minute. I need to bring clean sheets.'

It is not easy to find help when everyone is busy providing care. Donna can be a bit difficult sometimes, but she is not sitting in the lounge having a cup of tea. She is helping people and the tall carer does not want to be told to get lost twice. Dave is working in the other corridor and might be able to lend a hand for a few minutes. He is a big young man. He is also the worst of the lot when it comes to writing and the only one who cannot actually form the letters of the alphabet correctly. And, when it comes to hygiene, it is a similar story. He never uses gloves, doesn't wash his hands and then he'll offer you a cup of tea. No, thank you!

No one knows how he got hired to work in a care home and no one likes to work with him. He is a very sweet young man, though, always open and friendly, but there is this oddity about him. One day, he was helping with lunch, sitting at a table with the residents and other carers when he started describing how he had been sexually abused by his parents when he was a child. In his own universe, sexual abuse must be a normal topic for lunch-time conversation. Other times, his choice of conversation topics is just as misplaced[37].

'I hope you don't take me the wrong way but, how much do you spend on shopping every week? I mean food, groceries, house stuff. Excluding bills and rent, you know.'

'Why do you ask?'

'If I told you, you could save a whopping forty per cent on average, you wouldn't believe me, but it is true. And I can make it happen for you. Is it all right to talk about it? I mean, you don't mind, do you? I know we are at work and everything.'

'No, Dave. Go ahead.'

But Donna is coming down the corridor and Dave's sales pitch is interrupted.

---

[37] **Care Standards:** *19. Fit and proper persons employed.* (As in footnote 35 above).

'Elsie is dry, Albert is dry, Valery is dry. What's he doing here?' she asks looking at Dave.

'I need help with Norma. She has exploded,' replies the tall carer.

The tall carer suspects Elsie, Albert and Valery are lying in bed in wet pads. When the night shift take over, they will find them swimming in urine. But everyone has a different interpretation of time management and now Norma can have three carers to clear her faeces, give her a bed wash and change her sheets, and it is the senior carer, Donna, who leads the triad into Norma's room.

'Norma, what's your bell for?'

'I told you I needed a pad change.'

'So this is how you treat us! Why didn't you tell us, Norma? You must have known this was coming.'

'I told you…'

'The pad was dry when you told us! Really, Norma, you deserve to be left like that to rot in your own faeces!'

'Oh, don't do that.!'
'You are rude to us. Did you know that? You need to learn some manners. Look at what we'll have to clean now! I'm leaving you there like that. I am. Dave, you take care of this. Come on, Alex, I want to have a word with you.'

But let set four take care of set four. Valery is not in set four. She cannot walk. She cannot even sit up. She is in pain all day long, so she is on morphine. She is very quiet and polite and she never rings her bell. A person more resigned and accepting of her own fate could not be found in the home. Of course, everyone likes her, so she is definitely in set one. She is so set one she even has oil paintings of her houses and pets decorating her bedroom walls. She also has a photo album with people in suits, Italian lake holidays, and more pets. A little bit of silver here and there, and a fridge with her favourite drinks and treats. She gets her continence care and meals timely and with a smile. Valery is so nice and content there is not actually anything to say or write about her. And that is precisely the point. She will just die one day and no one will know. She will have a set one death, without disruption or fuss. But, in fact, Valery's set-one status is only lip service and she has also been getting the set-four treatment, so she is not really clean. Just like Norma, she now lies in a pond of urine and faeces. The thing is, once you have set four, it is set four for everyone.

©Alex Matthews 2018

Set 4

Eventually, Valery contracts infections both of the urinary tract and her mouth and throat. For days, she can't eat or drink anything. Valery says she's had enough, so medics and relatives agree to withhold medication. But nature is stubborn, so Valery will endure agony for five whole weeks. During these last days, Valery is responsive, so we can all say our good byes.

'Valery, do you really want to go? I'll miss you if you do.'

'I love you, I love you,' she repeats with a smile. *'Maybe she is taking me for her daughter,'* the tall carer thinks. Valery's only daughter is by her side a lot in the last days and the tall carer doesn't want to tell her that her mum's personal hygiene has systematically been neglected[38]. Valery had been complaining of a sore throat for months before a doctor was called in to see her. For months, the tall carer had reported the problems, but nothing was done about them. And why should anybody do anything about prolonging anybody's life? They come to the home not to live but to die. End of life care, they call it. Set four, more like.

You cannot tell nature which way to go, so after five weeks of agony on just water, Valery is still alive. Only then a course of antibiotics is prescribed. But Valery is in a bad way now. The smile is gone, she can still answer yes or no, but her eyes are vacant and with a sadness the tall carer has not seen before. There are no more grateful words from Valery, no more *I love yous*, perhaps because nobody deserves them.

It is too late for antibiotics, though. Valery will endure another two weeks of agony before going to that promised place. *'I'd like that,'* she had answered when the tall carer asked her if she wanted to go to Paradise. *'She was very strong,'* said the head nurse when she passed away. Indeed, seven weeks without eating is a hard exit. She must have been looking forward to Heaven. Let's just hope there isn't set four waiting for her over there too.

---

[38] **Care Standards:** *13. Safeguarding service users from abuse and improper treatment.* (1) Service users must be protected from abuse and improper treatment in accordance with this regulation. (2) Systems and processes must be established and operated effectively to prevent abuse of service users. (3) Systems and processes must be established and operated effectively to investigate, immediately upon becoming aware of, any allegation or evidence of such abuse. (4) Care or treatment for service users must not be provided in a way that— (a) includes discrimination against a service user on grounds of any protected characteristic (as defined in section 4 of the Equality Act 2010) of the service user, (b) includes acts intended to control or restrain a service user that are not necessary to prevent, or not a proportionate response to, a risk of harm posed to the service user or another individual if the service user was not subject to control or restraint, (c) is degrading for the service user, or (d) significantly disregards the needs of the service user for care or treatment.

©Alex Matthews 2018

Set 4

Set 4

Main point of advice

Intelligence gathering
This story shows a series of shortcomings with human resources and how the failure to hire fit and proper persons for the job affects people in a very negative way. In order to protect yourself or a relative from improper treatment, you'll need to gather intelligence about the care team. Talk to the carers and develop a psychological profile for each one. Talk to the other residents and their relatives and compare impressions. This vital intelligence will let you know who you should be avoiding. But be very diplomatic and subtle about your investigations: don't let anyone know who's on your black list lest the management of the home put you on their own black list. I know of a case where the daughter of a resident was punished with restricted access to the care home on the grounds that she was meddling. Let the care team know who you trust with your relative's care. It is often possible to choose the carers at least when they are on shift.

As you can see, once more, being physically there for your relative is key to preventing abuse.

Reflection points and positive advice you can offer to carers and managers

1. In this case, it is evident that the care home has not made an effort to hire the best workers for the job, clearly violating the standards in *Staffing* and in *Fit and proper persons employed*. What can the care industry do in order to address this problem?

Ideally, a care business should offer psychological, vocational and aptitudinal tests to all applicants, followed by good training and support. A system of incentives should be implemented based both on rewards as well as on career opportunities.

2. In this nursing home, proper processes and agreed ways of working are routinely sabotaged and a culture of non-compliance has been allowed to flourish. Why? What can be done to address some of the problems?

©Alex Matthews 2018

Set 4

The existence of a subculture of malpractice in the care home is due to three main problems: a deficient human resources strategy, poor training, and weak management.

Although low levels of staffing are affecting the moral of the workforce and having a negative impact on the clients, this is not necessarily the main issue. Rather, systematically hiring the wrong people for the job is the problem. An effective human resources strategy must be put into operation in order to solve this issue.

The home trainer is not mentioned in the case studies. One needs to read between the lines to realise that training in this nursing home is very poor. An inspiring leader should take on the job of training staff in order to give them both self-confidence and continuing support. Someone with the moral authority to show the way should be hired to do the job.

Lack of strong, inspiring leadership is the most important issue here. In the pages of *Abuse: The new normal?*, there is no mention of higher management. The manager is invisible. The nurses and care coordinators have been bulldozed by bullies and, as a result, carers are left to their own devices. The manager's presence must be felt. There is nothing more demoralising for the workforce than weak leadership. A management strategy is needed here including confident but approachable leaders, and a system that rewards good care and offers employees incentives to better themselves.

3. What are your thoughts on the end-of-life care offered to Valery? What might some of the problems be? Were they addressed timely and professionally?

We don't have all the medical details in order to draw any definite conclusions, but the reversal in the decision to stop medication is suspicious to say the least. If Valery's hygiene had been taken care of properly in the first place, this whole situation could have been avoided. So prevention could have been a proactive strategy in this case.

4. What can a new care worker do after they find themselves in a working environment where there is bullying and malpractice going on?

Officially, one is supposed to go to their line manager first. Failing that, there is a confidential whistleblowing telephone line provided by your employer, or one can contact the Care Quality Commission directly. The tall carer had no faith in the management of the nursing home or in the whistleblowing system. He did have informal conversations with care coordinators and nurses but, in the end, he decided to document the malpractice and contact the Care Quality Commission with all the details.

5. The tall carer checks Norma's pad and tells her that it is clean, that she can wait for a while. Was he being honest? What is happening to the tall carer? Is he going rogue?

Indeed, the tall carer is lying to Norma when he says that her pad is fine. *'It's a bit wet, but not too much. We'll come and change it for you in a few minutes.'* The tall carer is learning some bad habits from the other carers. He is going rogue. This is something that he avoids in the end by resigning from his job. But for a carer who does not want to quit at the first sign of trouble, a support structure that helps carers with their concerns should be in place so they feel confident enough to stand up to bullies and rogue carers. If this structure is not in place where you work, you should be quite worried.

6. In a working environment with huge time pressures, how can one make sure that every single client gets proper hygiene?

This problem should really be addressed by management. There is little a carer can do in this case apart from insisting to the manager that more carers are needed in order to do the job properly. In any case, carers should never feel pressured to do their job so quickly that doing it properly becomes impossible.

7. Many things seem to go wrong with Valery's end-of-life care. What are some of them? How would you feel about witnessing such unprofessional care?

Even though the case study shows unprofessional end-of-life care, it was probably arranged following proper standard procedures. When the palliative-care-only orders are reversed, we can only suspect that something is wrong, but that might not necessarily be the case. There could be a perfectly good reason for reversing such orders. Only the relatives, nurses and doctors involved know what really went on. However, it was not fair on carers to have to witness the end-of-life process without being informed about all the details. Keeping the carers in the dark caused them unnecessary grief and stress.

Smeared Pages

It is breakfast time in the dementia unit and the residents are being brought into the dining room. Those in the very advanced stages of the condition arrive in comfortable made-to-order arm chairs and do not sit at tables. They rest in frozen poses with vacant expressions in their eyes. Paul is sitting next to the window. According to his life history album, he had been a long distance lorry driver, a roofer, a beer bottle collector, and he loved going down the pub. His care is paid for by the National Health Service, so he is very lucky to have ended up in such a good private care home. He has one arm up in the air. Is he ordering a pint? His friend Tom is sitting at a table because he can still walk. He is also in the advanced stages of dementia.

They used to hang out together a lot when they first came to the home and they still greet each other without uttering a word, just a look of recognition. Viv was a very good painter. Her artwork is on display in her bedroom and much admired by everyone. When she was diagnosed with dementia, her husband dumped her in the care home and never came back. He is currently with another woman and perfunctorily sends his wife the clothes and toiletries she needs. Vivien never gets visits. She is permanently locked into a foetal position with her knees right up against her chest and she sits dangerously in that position.

Harry arrives now to join the advanced dementia group. He made it through the ranks in The Royal Navy before joining a merchant fleet as a captain. But he was also a country lad. He spent the first few years of retirement taking care of a small farm. He sits with his back really straight in his hi-tech chair. His eyes tell us he is in a different world; his mouth slightly open as if he had just remembered to say something only to forget what he actually meant to say. If the members of this group move at all, they do it like new-born babies, in jerky motions, unable to control their strength. Puppets who've lost their strings.

Their condition is terrible, but at least they are in a high-end care home. They all get a good bed wash in the morning. They are treated humanely even though they can't remember who they are, and they are given choices even if they can't make up their minds. A big effort is always made to preserve their dignity, so every care action performed is explained to them in spite of the fact that they may not be able to understand a word. And now they will be assisted to eat a full English breakfast cooked by a proper chef and served by trained carers.

Enter Kath now, pushed by a smiley girl. Kath is wearing her hair up in a trendy doughnut. She had been a music teacher, but you would never guess

©Alex Matthews 2018

it judging by the way she ignores Bob Marley's *Satisfy my Soul*. The dementia unit has been carefully decorated to resemble a real home. There is even an element of careful untidiness: memorabilia strewn around here and there, magazines, CDs. Yes, lots of music. There are radios tuned to different stations in every corner of the unit. The Bob Marley song is over and Lynyrd Skynrd's *Free Bird* is playing now. But this is really too much for a senior carer who disapproves of the long-winded guitar solo and moves to the radio, and selects a classical music programme. Kath's cup of tea no doubt but, no reaction.

Breakfast arrives in a hot trolley and the one-to-one carers are in charge of dishing out and assisting people. The other carers are still busy getting the last residents up and bringing them into the main dining room. Malcolm, Elsie, Daphne and other relatively able residents arrive on foot or pushed in normal wheelchairs and they share elegantly laid tables. But everyone must be *'done'* before breakfast, so they arrive looking less trendy and more dishevelled as the deadline approaches.

Classical music is all about variation and progression. Now some of the carers are getting restless as they cannot stand the sophistication of pieces that go on for longer than three minutes, without a hi-hat. So one of them turns the dial to a simple jingle with a strong beat. Not only do some of the residents take notice of the music now, some of them are even nodding to the rhythm, smiling and looking around for smiles. Who would have guessed. Most experts recommend classical, not house, especially at meal times.

Everyone is in the dining room now, including the nurse, who has finished her morning round. She has a heaped plate of food in front of her, enough to feed several people, but you do get hungry when you start at seven in the morning. Her face is on her breakfast, so she does not notice the growing dribble on some of the residents' faces. Or maybe she does, but her own food is more important at the moment[39].

---

[39] **Care Standards:** *17. Good governance.* (1) Systems or processes must be established and operated effectively to ensure compliance with the requirements in this Part. (2) Without limiting paragraph (1), such systems or processes must enable the registered person, in particular, to— (a) assess, monitor and improve the quality and safety of the services provided in the carrying on of the regulated activity (including the quality of the experience of service users in receiving those services); (b) assess, monitor and mitigate the risks relating to the health, safety and welfare of service users and others who may be at risk which arise from the carrying on of the regulated activity; (c) maintain securely an accurate, complete and contemporaneous record in respect of each service user, including a record of the care and treatment provided to the service user and of decisions taken in relation to the care and treatment provided; (d) maintain securely such other records as are necessary to be kept in relation to— (i) persons employed in the carrying on of the regulated activity, and (ii) the management of the regulated activity; (e) seek and act

The atmosphere is quite lively now. All the staff are busy helping around. The pounding music is still on. While the residents are fairly quiet, there is carer gossip at the tables. Personal details that one would not wish to know about are aired. Are they really comparing sexual performance at the table? There is general laughter. Are the hens out of the coop? But the tall man is not amused at all. The carers are feeding two or more residents at the same time, so now the picture is one of faces smeared in porridge.

When the tall carer saw Trish for the first time, sitting in the lounge, staring into space, he thought she must be a resident. A young one. Only we don't admit young residents here. After a few weeks working with her, his first impression is confirmed: she is not really there at all. He has seen her in town with her husband and two beautiful young sons. A picture of a perfect family. But the way she behaves in the care home points to some deep personal problem. She hardly ever talks to anyone, not even to say *'hello'*. She doesn't use gloves when she is toileting residents or changing pads. She does not communicate about the actions that she is performing, as if the residents were objects. She has been working at the home for ten years so there is really no excuse for the way she carries on[40].

She is now pushing porridge, big spoonfuls of it, into Harry's mouth on one side and into Vivien's on the other. Only Viv is not opening her mouth, so Trish is pushing that metallic spoon against Viv's teeth and the porridge spills all over the place. She is not the only carer doing a lousy job of feeding people but she is the worst. The spoon goes again against the teeth and the porridge dribbles down Viv's face and onto her bib. The tall carer wants to say something about it but this happens every morning and no one ever complains; besides, he is fairly new in the care home and it isn't his place to tell senior workers how to do their jobs. Why doesn't the nurse say anything?

---

on feedback from relevant persons and other persons on the services provided in the carrying on of the regulated activity, for the purposes of continually evaluating and improving such services; (f) evaluate and improve their practice in respect of the processing of the information referred to in sub-paragraphs (a) to (e).

[40] **Care Standards:** *19. Fit and proper persons employed.* (1) Persons employed for the purposes of carrying on a regulated activity must— (a) be of good character, (b) have the qualifications, competence, skills and experience which are necessary for the work to be performed by them, and (c) be able by reason of their health, after reasonable adjustments are made, of properly performing tasks which are intrinsic to the work for which they are employed. (2) Recruitment procedures must be established and operated effectively to ensure that persons employed meet the conditions in— (a) paragraph (1), or (b) in a case to which regulation 5 applies, paragraph (3) of that regulation. (3) The following information must be available in relation to each such person employed— (a) the information specified in Schedule 3, and (b) such other information as is required under any enactment to be kept by the registered person in relation to such persons employed.

But she is enthralled in her own food orgy. The tall carer decides to wipe Vivien's face and change her bib without uttering a word. There is something red on Vivien's lips. He is truly disgusted now and makes Trish aware of the situation. *'Is this blood?'* He wonders if this is supposed to be normal. If he is the only one who cares[41].

The tall man feels as if he were reading the last pages of people's life history albums. Stories that always end on a stretcher and out of the front door of the care home. He is realising that he is sharing resident's lives in a very fundamental way: he is trying to understand what they are going through and, in the process, he is getting drawn into the residents' conditions. He suffers with them and cries when that last page is read. And he is learning something about human nature. The tall carer has been thinking a lot about what makes us human since he started working in the dementia unit. They probably still teach school children that what makes us human is our ability to think logically, to understand, remember and act upon information that is available to us. Others will tell you that it is the way we use science, technology and the arts in order to create societies where we can live in a civilised manner. Still others will claim it is our connection with God that makes us human. Whatever it is, the residents in the dementia unit have lost the ability to engage in any of that. They don't even know who they are. Some of them don't even feel pain anymore. But they are still human.

---

[41] **Care Standards:** *13. Safeguarding service users from abuse and improper treatment.* (1) Service users must be protected from abuse and improper treatment in accordance with this regulation. (2) Systems and processes must be established and operated effectively to prevent abuse of service users. (3) Systems and processes must be established and operated effectively to investigate, immediately upon becoming aware of, any allegation or evidence of such abuse. (4) Care or treatment for service users must not be provided in a way that— (a) includes discrimination against a service user on grounds of any protected characteristic (as defined in section 4 of the Equality Act 2010) of the service user, (b) includes acts intended to control or restrain a service user that are not necessary to prevent, or not a proportionate response to, a risk of harm posed to the service user or another individual if the service user was not subject to control or restraint, (c) is degrading for the service user, or (d) significantly disregards the needs of the service user for care or treatment. (5) A service user must not be deprived of their liberty for the purpose of receiving care or treatment without lawful authority. (6) For the purposes of this regulation— "abuse" means— (a) any behaviour towards a service user that is an offence under the Sexual Offences Act 2003(a), (b) ill-treatment (whether of a physical or psychological nature) of a service user, (c) theft, misuse or misappropriation of money or property belonging to a service user, or (d) neglect of a service user. (7) For the purposes of this regulation, a person controls or restrains a service user if that person— (a) uses, or threatens to use, force to secure the doing of an act which the service user resists, or (b) restricts the service user's liberty of movement, whether or not the service user resists, including by use of physical, mechanical or chemical means.

©Alex Matthews 2018

Smeared Pages

While the tall carer wondered about the meaning of humanness, Trish was at it again and now even Harry's beard is smeared in dribble, only he can't stop drawing his hands to his face and hair, so he is covering himself in breakfast. Also Paul, and Kath as well as Tom and quite a few of the residents at the tables are sitting with some degree of dribble on their faces. And the tall man is getting depressed not only about the dribble – the carers are now sharing the left-over breakfast and making lewd comments about the sausages in the hot trolley.

Happiness? Or, rather, the pursuit of happiness? Is that what makes us human? Or is it the ability to love? No. That is also gone here and yet our clients are still human. The tall carer feels there could be no one as human as the people he cares for. Even if their heads are covered in porridge and they don't even realise it. So he has reached the conclusion that what makes us human must be extrinsic, outside of every one of us. When it comes to the residents, especially those with advanced dementia, what makes them human is the way we treat them. It is every step taken in order to protect that very humanity. From the state, who provides them with protection in the form of legislation, inspecting bodies, and funding. To care providers, who go the extra mile to ensure that their clients live in pleasant surroundings, eat good food, and get all the care and choice they deserve. To each and every carer who do their best to make sure that the people they care for are safe and respected. To the family members who come and visit in spite of the fact that they are no longer recognised. That is what makes all of us human, the way we treat each other and regard each other as human. That, and our respect for basic human rights. So when a carer asks someone who cannot answer, or even understand, whether they want to wear blue or green, they are regarding the person as human. When we cover a resident's body with towels during personal care even though they can't really see (or mind, in some cases) what is happening to them, carers are respecting the dignity and humanness of their clients.

But now we are looking at Harry's life history album and new pictures emerge. Pictures of him sitting in his Franciscan pose, his beard and hair smeared in porridge. There are new photos in Vivien's album too. A defenceless old woman, sitting in a foetal position trying to protect herself, her face covered in porridge and blood. Paul too. He never got his pint, but a covering of porridge all over his face and apron. And there are new pictures in Tom's book too, as in Paul's, Kath's, Malcolm's and many more. In their books we now see pictures of neglect, because when porridge gets smeared on someone's face and no one says anything about it, we are depriving them of their human qualities. We are failing to provide the quality of care that people expect. The last pages of our residents' lives become smeared pages[42].

---

[42] **Code of Conduct 2:** *Promote and uphold the privacy, dignity, rights, health and wellbeing of people who use health and care services and their carers at all times.*

©Alex Matthews 2018

As a Healthcare Support Worker or Adult Social Care Worker in England you must: 1. always act in the best interests of people who use health and care services. 2. always treat people with respect and compassion. 3. put the needs, goals and aspirations of people who use health and care services first, helping them to be in control and to choose the healthcare, care and support they receive. 4. promote people's independence and ability to self-care, assisting those who use health and care services to exercise their rights and make informed choices. 5. always gain valid consent before providing healthcare, care and support. You must also respect a person's right to refuse to receive healthcare, care and support if they are capable of doing so. 6. always maintain the privacy and dignity of people who use health and care services, their carers and others. 7. be alert to any changes that could affect a person's needs or progress and report your observations in line with your employer's agreed ways of working. 8. always make sure that your actions or omissions do not harm an individual's health or wellbeing. You must never abuse, neglect, harm or exploit those who use health and care services, their carers or your colleagues. 9. challenge and report dangerous, abusive, discriminatory or exploitative behaviour or practice.

©Alex Matthews 2018

Main point of advice

Laxity

In this story, we find carers and a nurse who have given up on doing a good job. They don't believe in themselves anymore. The malpractice of smearing porridge on residents' faces is so widespread that every single carer is engaged in it. As a result, the residents' dignity is severely compromised. In fact, it wouldn't take more effort or time to do the job properly. This points to the management problem already mentioned in previous chapters: the managers are nowhere to be seen. And the nurse is so disempowered that she couldn't care less. Unfortunately, you will not be able to enforce management presence and carer supervision on the floor. But you can make yourself visible by visiting your relative at meal times. Again, if you cannot visit often enough, try to find an advocate for your relative in the care system. It won't be easy to convince the carers to do a clean job of helping your relative with their meal. They will complain and try to bar you from the dining room – I have seen this with my very own eyes. But carers are not bad people, and they will be glad that someone is trying to raise care standards, even if they complain about your meddling.

Reflection points and positive advice you can offer to carers and managers

1. In this case, we find a nurse who does not care. Not only that, she seems to have developed some unhealthy eating habits. What factors might have influenced this nurse's improper behaviour?

One can only assume that the nurse has not been empowered by the management of the nursing home. She does not want to face the carers. That's why she buries her face in her plate. The fact that she needs to eat huge amounts of food could point to her need for self-gratification which, in turn, reveals the lack of incentives and appreciation of her hard work. While her behaviour is absolutely objectionable, this really points to the wider issue of poor management that the nursing home is facing.

2. What are your thoughts on the training of the carers in this case study?

As we have seen in previous case studies in this book, there seems to be a training and supervision problem at this nursing home. Together with the nurse, Trish is another case of a worker who seems to have lost her enthusiasm to perform her best. It is of paramount importance to bring an inspirational leading and training team to the home.

3. In spite of all the problems, this seems to be a good care home where an effort is being made to comply with the Fundamental Care Standards and the European Charter of Human Rights. It is clear that a few crucial mistakes are being made that allow some malpractice to take place. What are these mistakes and how could they be addressed? Think about human resources, training, and management.

This question has been answered at some length in *Set 4*, question 2. Perhaps one needs to stress again how important it is to get everything right one hundred percent of the time when it comes to people's health and wellbeing. The tone of this case study is ironic. It contrasts exemplary care, which is probably the norm at this nursing home, with the appalling care also taking place. What we learn is that just making an effort is never enough when it comes to caring for vulnerable service users.

4. What seems to be the problem with Trish? Can she get help?

We don't know what the problem is with Trish, but we can make some educated guesses. We have learned about the poor training and lack of proper supervision at the home. We have also read about bullying and lack of support. Trish is probably demoralised and does not remember the importance of her role any more. She has become a mindless robot pushing spoonfuls of food into people's mouths. Trish has worked at the nursing home for many years, and we learn that no-one likes to work with her, so we can also suspect that nobody in the leadership team notices or cares about her problem.

5. What code of conduct is Trish breaking?

Indirectly, Trish is breaking almost every single code there is, but mainly she is breaking the second code of conduct (see Appendix 2).

True Love

The tall carer is seven years old. He lives in a small village in the foothills of a mountain range. He is selecting the best flowers in his garden for Great Aunt Modestina. She lives in the municipal care home a short walk from the boy's house. Modestina never got married, so she has no children of her own to take care of her. But she took care of almost everyone else in the boy's extended family before she went blind. So Modestina is a much loved and respected member of the family.

The skinny boy loves taking her flowers. Picking them and making a bouquet is fun. Another thing he likes is to be warmly greeted by the nuns who run the facility. Then there is the grown-up feeling of walking by himself along the corridors all the way to Modestina's room, along with the mysterious monastic smell emanating from the chapel, a mixture of incense and candle wax, so potent and special. And, of course, giving her the flowers and receiving a magnificent five peseta tip. Modestina cannot see and the boy loves being her eyes. He helps her find things around her room and often takes her to the garden. They just sit together in the sunshine for ages and that makes him feel great. But, of course, it isn't just the sunshine.

Five pesetas can buy a fair amount of sweets but not too many, so his visits to Aunty Modestina take place rather frequently. He can find flowers in the garden all year round, which means that supply is not a problem.

Aunty Modestina comes home for lunch on Sundays. The boy loves to have her over and be her guide. The house is huge and full of dangers, so they need to be really careful when they walk from one place to another. The carer boy feels great to be entrusted with this responsibility. He feels important. At lunch time, he sits next to Modestina and she always gets seconds. *'Why do they force her to eat?'* he wonders. And he doesn't like the way the adults sometimes make jokes and talk about things she cannot see. That makes her feel confused. After the meal and siesta are over, the proud boy escorts Modestina back to the care home.

It is only forty years ago, but it feels like a different era, a very different world. People do their grocery shopping every day and get fresh produce. That means that the pantry is always empty. But it also means that the village has a good supply of small corner shops where goodies can be bought. So the boy puts together a bunch of flowers and walks to the care home to get his five pesetas. Only, this time, Aunty Modestina does not reach for her little purse. And, strangely, the boy feels liberated. Free from a guilty feeling that he had been getting. And he suddenly realises that he loves Aunty Modestina. He loved her before, of course, but only now does he realise that he is not giving the flowers for money. It is love. It is true love that he has just discovered. So, from now on, he will enjoy taking flowers to Modestina just for the love of it.

It is forty years ago and people do not lock front doors. Sometimes they even leave them open. So Cousin Mari Paz is able to barge in and run up the stairs screaming *'Aunty Modestina has died'* at the top of her voice. The boy feels his heart break. He spends the rest of the day crying. Mum brings him olives as a treat and tells him that aunty Modestina is not dead. It was a stroke.

Days later, aunty Modestina does eventually die but all the tears had been shed the day Mari Paz announced her death. The carer boy cannot cry now. He just scribbles Modestina's name everywhere, in his school books and on the walls. Modestina has taken a place in the boy's heart and there she will live. For ever. And when, forty years later, he takes care of someone at the home, Modestina is right there, by his side, as an ever present inspiration.

True Love

Main reflection point

Vocation
This story shows how vocation and good care go hand-in-hand. When you talk to the carers, try to discover what made them choose their job. This will add to your psychological profiling and will help you make up your mind about who the best carers are.

But this story is also about a care home resident who gets frequent visits and is taken out regularly. This is an important care element that is often missing in care homes: too many people are just parked there, far away from family, cut off from the wider community. As I have mentioned in every single case study, having advocates who can speak up for the residents is key to stopping abuse from happening.

Epilogue

There is an air of spring about, as the song goes. The days are longer, the blood runs faster and there is an anticipation of walks in the park, bicycle rides, barbecues, and fun. But for the residents at the care home it might as well be winter all through the year.

Martha's daughters come to visit when they can, which is seldom. She has no interest in reading, listening to the radio, or watching television. She cannot hear perfectly, so she sometimes misinterprets what is said to her, and she is often seen arguing with other residents in a conference of the deaf. Sometimes she even thinks people talk behind her back and that sends her into a frantic state; she will then break down and accuse other people of trying to harm her. To make things worse, she sometimes forgets that she cannot walk.

But she can also be happy and friendly.

'The Kind Giant? Who's that, Martha?'

'You are. You must have told me your name a hundred times before, but I remember you as the Kind Giant.'

'I like that. Thank you. I really like that,' replies the tall carer.

That was a while ago, though. Martha is now sitting in the atrium with the other residents. She is not looking very happy and there is definitely no air of spring about her. The tall carer is looking at Martha trying not to be seen by her. He knows that Martha can relax a bit when he is around. Most of the other carers are fed up with her and just tell her to shut up which makes Martha feel worthless and rejected[43]. The tall carer can sit next to Martha and make her feel better with just a smile. But he is really busy right now and

---

[43] **Care Standards:** *19. Fit and proper persons employed.* (1) Persons employed for the purposes of carrying on a regulated activity must— (a) be of good character, (b) have the qualifications, competence, skills and experience which are necessary for the work to be performed by them, and (c) be able by reason of their health, after reasonable adjustments are made, of properly performing tasks which are intrinsic to the work for which they are employed. (2) Recruitment procedures must be established and operated effectively to ensure that persons employed meet the conditions in— (a) paragraph (1), or (b) in a case to which regulation 5 applies, paragraph (3) of that regulation. (3) The following information must be available in relation to each such person employed— (a) the information specified in Schedule 3, and (b) such other information as is required under any enactment to be kept by the registered person in relation to such persons employed.

©Alex Matthews 2018

he knows that by the time he can go to Martha it will be too late; she will already be in tears. This is very frustrating for him.

It is so annoying that the tall carer has had enough and has handed in his notice. He is basically a quitter. Unlike Jessica, the only person in the home the tall carer looks up to. Jess has been working at the home for a few years now. She is always correct. She will never be heard cracking a silly joke or telling anyone to shut up. Because she is dead serious about care, and this shows in her demeanour. She is serious but approachable. She can make everyone feel safe and appreciated. And it must be frustrating for her too to work with a bunch of amateurs, to realise that she cannot reach out to everyone who needs her. But she is not quitting. That is not the answer. Florence Nightingale did not give up at the first sign of trouble during the Crimean War. Jess is a true bearer of Nightingale's spirit and she knows that she can make a difference.

But the tall carer is not following in Nightingale's footsteps. Yes, he has earned everyone's respect, including residents and staff. Some senior carers have even complemented him that he is an inspiration to all. And he is due for promotion. But he is still giving up. He has been pacing up and down that dementia unit corridor too many times, feeling an eerie connection with the residents that populate it; making eye contact with them; becoming one of them. He has been frustrated at having to tell residents that he couldn't stay a minute to chat with them when he knew well that they needed it more than medicine. Alas, a care home is not a good place for an idealist. Maybe that is the difference between him and Jess.

But enough with the excuses, Kind Giant, you may be an idealist, but you are also a cheat. You can have all the spring air you like while the people you have been caring for will continue to die a little every day as they endure their private winter of powerlessness and isolation.

Unless you write about them and give them a voice: warn people that the care we give our loved ones can be brutal sometimes. Perhaps that will help their cause[44].

---

[44] The tall carer eventually disclosed the malpractice described in these pages to the Care Quality Commission.

©Alex Matthews 2018

Epilogue

Main point of advice

This is another clear case of neglect due to short staffing. This story also reflects the frustration and lack of support that carers have to endure, which lead to carers eventually leaving their jobs and the people they have come to love. High levels of staff turnover is another of the scourges in the care industry. A vicious circle where the recruitment process is not thorough and new carers are seldom fit and proper persons; then, lack of carer support and work overload, leading to carer frustration and resignations.

When you or your relative enter the care system, you can expect to see many new faces taking care of you. The only way to alleviate this lack of continuity in your support is to at least get some family members coming to visit you regularly.

Reflection points and positive advice you can offer to carers and managers

1. What fundamental standard needs to be addressed in order to tackle Martha's isolation?

Mainly the standards in *Person centred care* (Regulation 9). The home has to devise a strategy in order to address Martha's communication needs and help lessen her sense of isolation.

2. Once again, we find carers being rude to service users. What can be done to improve carers' manners?

There are three main things to consider: hiring fit and proper persons for the job is the first. Offering inspiring training and supervision is also important here. Finally, it is necessary to give carers enough time to do their jobs. Failing that, care homes could arrange to invite volunteers to have chats over a cup of tea with their residents. That way, the carers could focus more on the core tasks of personal care, personal hygiene, moving and handling, assisting with meals, and documenting the care they have provided.

©Alex Matthews 2018

3. Powerlessness and isolation describe the general state of the residents at this nursing home. Are these conditions not inherent to the aging process anyway?

It could be argued that we all lose power and miss out on socialising opportunities as we age, but care providers are bound by the legislation laid out in the Care Act to provide person centred care, and protect the dignity and respect of service users, in particular *'supporting the autonomy, independence and involvement in the community of the service user'* as we learn in *Dignity and respect*, Regulation 10, clause 2.b. But also care providers need to *safeguard service users from abuse and improper treatment* (Regulation 13). Basically, if the care provider leaves a vulnerable person unattended to the point of causing the person to become so upset that they will break into tears, then the service provider is breaking the law. So, powerlessness and isolation should be properly addressed by care providers at all costs.

4. In a previous story, the tall carer tells us about his early vocation as a child-carer. Here we learn that he is not following in Florence Nightingale's footsteps. Basically, he is contradicting himself. Or is he? In your opinion, why is he giving up?

Whether it is neglect, or abuse, or bullying, or malpractice, there isn't a single day when the tall carer can enjoy his job without having to witness something unpleasant. There is too much hidden neglect in this care home for him to bear. In the introduction to this book I mentioned a 2018 UCL survey where neglect was experienced by fifty per cent of respondents in ninety nine percent of the care homes where it was carried out. The UCL study is a sad confirmation of the testimony provided in the case studies presented in this book and it explains the high carer turnover in care homes.

©Alex Matthews 2018

Conclusion

The care we give our older adults can be brutal, that's true. Through the stories presented in this book, we have seen how underfunding in social care leads to cuts in care services resulting in care homes not having enough hands to support their residents in an efficient, caring and safe way. The State could do much more in terms of funding in order to improve the care system but, will they? At the time of writing we are in 2019. The United Kingdom prides itself on being the fifth economic power in the world and yet, every week the media informs us about cases of elder abuse. So, unless we also want to compete in a league with the most uncaring and uncompassionate countries in the world, the fifth economic power should put more financial resources in taking care of what's left of the generation that rebuilt this country from the ashes of the Blitz.

But, as we have seen in the reflection sections of this book, improving standards of care is not only up to the State, or the CQC, or the care companies, but you. You need to be there for your relative in the care system. For now, at least, your presence and advocacy will be the most important element in safeguarding your relative in a care system that abuses its own users by default.

©Alex Matthews 2018

Appendix 1 – The Fundamental Care Standards

The *Fundamental Care Standards* are a section of the *Care Act 2008*. The original text can be found at *The Health and Social Care Act 2008 (Regulated Activities) Regulations, Part 3*, available from Guv.uk. The version used here is the 2014 one. This legislation was amended in 2015 but the 2014 version is fit for the purposes of this care guide. The fundamental care standards are an instrument of law used by the *Care Quality Commission* in order regulate the care industry.

The Fundamental Standards are also used as the foundation for the *Care Certificate* (See http://www.skillsforcare.org.uk/ for further information on the Certificate standards).

The legislation provided in this appendix is protected by Crown Copyright and is reproduced herein under the rules set out by the Open Government Licence. This document may be used only for learning and training purposes.

Users are not permitted to use this legislation in any way that will distort or change its original intention or meaning.

The legislation provided here is for reference only, and is not to be used as a substitute for the exercise of professional judgement or legal advice.

Last updated: 22 November 2018

STATUTORY INSTRUMENTS

2014 No. 2936

NATIONAL HEALTH SERVICE, ENGLAND

SOCIAL CARE, ENGLAND

PUBLIC HEALTH, ENGLAND

The Health and Social Care Act 2008 (Regulated Activities) Regulations 2014

©Crown Copyright

Appendix 1

Made - - - - 6th November 2014

[...]

PART 3, SECTION 2 Fundamental Standards

8. General

(1) A registered person must comply with regulations 9 to 19 in carrying on a regulated activity.

(2) But paragraph (1) does not require a person to do something to the extent that what is required to be done to comply with regulations 9 to 19 has already been done by another person who is a registered person in relation to the regulated activity concerned.

(3) For the purposes of determining under regulations 9 to 19 whether a service user who is 16 or over lacks capacity, sections 2 and 3 of the 2005 Act (people who lack capacity) apply as they apply for the purposes of that Act.

9. Person-centred care

(1) The care and treatment of service users must—

    (a) be appropriate,

    (b) meet their needs, and

    (c) reflect their preferences.

(2) But paragraph (1) does not apply to the extent that the provision of care or treatment would result in a breach of regulation 11.

(3) Without limiting paragraph (1), the things which a registered person must do to comply with that paragraph include—

©Crown Copyright

(a) carrying out, collaboratively with the relevant person, an assessment of the needs and preferences for care and treatment of the service user;

(b) designing care or treatment with a view to achieving service users' preferences and ensuring their needs are met;

(c) enabling and supporting relevant persons to understand the care or treatment choices available to the service user and to discuss, with a competent health care professional or other competent person, the balance of risks and benefits involved in any particular course of treatment;

(d) enabling and supporting relevant persons to make, or participate in making, decisions relating to the service user's care or treatment to the maximum extent possible;

(e) providing opportunities for relevant persons to manage the service user's care or treatment;

(f) involving relevant persons in decisions relating to the way in which the regulated activity is carried on in so far as it relates to the service user's care or treatment;

(g) providing relevant persons with the information they would reasonably need for the purposes of sub-paragraphs (c) to (f);

(h) making reasonable adjustments to enable the service user to receive their care or treatment;

(i) where meeting a service user's nutritional and hydration needs, having regard to the service user's well-being.

(4) Paragraphs (1) and (3) apply subject to paragraphs (5) and (6).

(5) If the service user is 16 or over and lacks capacity in relation to a matter to which this regulation applies, paragraphs (1) to (3) are subject to any duty on the registered person under the 2005 Act in relation to that matter.

(6) But if Part 4 or 4A of the 1983 Act applies to a service user, care and treatment must be provided in accordance with the provisions of that Act.

©Crown Copyright

Appendix 1

10. Dignity and respect

(1) Service users must be treated with dignity and respect.

(2) Without limiting paragraph (1), the things which a registered person is required to do to comply with paragraph (1) include in particular—

> (a) ensuring the privacy of the service user;
>
> (b) supporting the autonomy, independence and involvement in the community of the service user;
>
> (c) having due regard to any relevant protected characteristics (as defined in section 149(7) of the Equality Act 2010) of the service user.

11. Need for consent

(1) Care and treatment of service users must only be provided with the consent of the relevant person.

(2) Paragraph (1) is subject to paragraphs (3) and (4).

(3) If the service user is 16 or over and is unable to give such consent because they lack capacity to do so, the registered person must act in accordance with the 2005 Act.

(4) But if Part 4 or 4A of the 1983 Act applies to a service user, the registered person must act in accordance with the provisions of that Act.

(5) Nothing in this regulation affects the operation of section 5 of the 2005 Act, as read with section 6 of that Act (acts in connection with care or treatment).

12. Safe care and treatment

(1) Care and treatment must be provided in a safe way for service users.

(2) Without limiting paragraph (1), the things which a registered person must do to comply with that paragraph include—

©Crown Copyright

Appendix 1

(a) assessing the risks to the health and safety of service users of receiving the care or treatment;

(b) doing all that is reasonably practicable to mitigate any such risks;

(c) ensuring that persons providing care or treatment to service users have the qualifications, competence, skills and experience to do so safely;

(d) ensuring that the premises used by the service provider are safe to use for their intended purpose and are used in a safe way;

(e) ensuring that the equipment used by the service provider for providing care or treatment to a service user is safe for such use and is used in a safe way;

(f) where equipment or medicines are supplied by the service provider, ensuring that there are sufficient quantities of these to ensure the safety of service users and to meet their needs;

(g) the proper and safe management of medicines;

(h) assessing the risk of, and preventing, detecting and controlling the spread of, infections, including those that are health care associated;

(i) where responsibility for the care and treatment of service users is shared with, or transferred to, other persons, working with such other persons, service users and other appropriate persons to ensure that timely care planning takes place to ensure the health, safety and welfare of the service users.

13. Safeguarding service users from abuse and improper treatment

(1) Service users must be protected from abuse and improper treatment in accordance with this regulation.

(2) Systems and processes must be established and operated effectively to prevent abuse of service users.

©Crown Copyright

Appendix 1

(3) Systems and processes must be established and operated effectively to investigate, immediately upon becoming aware of, any allegation or evidence of such abuse.

(4) Care or treatment for service users must not be provided in a way that—

> (a) includes discrimination against a service user on grounds of any protected characteristic (as defined in section 4 of the Equality Act 2010) of the service user,
>
> (b) includes acts intended to control or restrain a service user that are not necessary to prevent, or not a proportionate response to, a risk of harm posed to the service user or another individual if the service user was not subject to control or restraint,
>
> (c) is degrading for the service user, or
>
> (d) significantly disregards the needs of the service user for care or treatment.

(5) A service user must not be deprived of their liberty for the purpose of receiving care or treatment without lawful authority.

(6) For the purposes of this regulation— "abuse" means—

> (a) any behaviour towards a service user that is an offence under the Sexual Offences Act 2003(a),
>
> (b) ill-treatment (whether of a physical or psychological nature) of a service user,
>
> (c) theft, misuse or misappropriation of money or property belonging to a service user, or
>
> (d) neglect of a service user.

(7) For the purposes of this regulation, a person controls or restrains a service user if that person—

> (a) uses, or threatens to use, force to secure the doing of an act which the service user resists, or

©Crown Copyright

Appendix 1

(b) restricts the service user's liberty of movement, whether or not the service user resists, including by use of physical, mechanical or chemical means.

14. Meeting nutritional and hydration needs

(1) The nutritional and hydration needs of service users must be met.

(2) Paragraph (1) applies where—

(a) care or treatment involves—

(i) the provision of accommodation by the service provider, or

(ii) an overnight stay for the service user on premises used by the service for the purposes of carrying on a regulated activity, or

(b) the meeting of the nutritional or hydration needs of service users is part of the arrangements made for the provision of care or treatment by the service provider.

(3) But paragraph (1) does not apply to the extent that the meeting of such nutritional or hydration needs would—

(a) result in a breach of regulation 11, or

(b) not be in the service user's best interests.

(4) For the purposes of paragraph (1), "nutritional and hydration needs" means—

(a) receipt by a service user of suitable and nutritious food and hydration which is adequate to sustain life and good health,

(b) receipt by a service user of parenteral nutrition and dietary supplements when prescribed by a health care professional,

(c) the meeting of any reasonable requirements of a service user for food and hydration arising from the service user's preferences or their religious or cultural background, and

(d) if necessary, support for a service user to eat or drink.

©Crown Copyright

Appendix 1

(5) Section 4 of the 2005 Act (best interests) applies for the purposes of determining the best interests of a service user who is 16 or over under this regulation as it applies for the purposes of that Act.

15. Premises and equipment

(1) All premises and equipment used by the service provider must be—

(a) clean,

(b) secure,

(c) suitable for the purpose for which they are being used,

(d) properly used,

(e) properly maintained, and

(f) appropriately located for the purpose for which they are being used.

(2) The registered person must, in relation to such premises and equipment, maintain standards of hygiene appropriate for the purposes for which they are being used.

(3) For the purposes of paragraph (1)(b), (c), (e) and (f), "equipment" does not include equipment at the service user's accommodation if—

(a) such accommodation is not provided as part of the service user's care or treatment, and

(b) such equipment is not supplied by the service provider.

16. Receiving and acting on complaints

(1) Any complaint received must be investigated and necessary and proportionate action must be taken in response to any failure identified by the complaint or investigation.

(2) The registered person must establish and operate effectively an accessible system for identifying, receiving, recording, handling and

Appendix 1

responding to complaints by service users and other persons in relation to the carrying on of the regulated activity.

(3) The registered person must provide to the Commission, when requested to do so and by no later than 28 days beginning on the day after receipt of the request, a summary of—

(a) complaints made under such complaints system,

(b) responses made by the registered person to such complaints and any further correspondence with the complainants in relation to such complaints, and

(c) any other relevant information in relation to such complaints as the Commission may request.

17. Good governance

(1) Systems or processes must be established and operated effectively to ensure compliance with the requirements in this Part.

(2) Without limiting paragraph (1), such systems or processes must enable the registered person, in particular, to—

(a) assess, monitor and improve the quality and safety of the services provided in the carrying on of the regulated activity (including the quality of the experience of service users in receiving those services);

(b) assess, monitor and mitigate the risks relating to the health, safety and welfare of service users and others who may be at risk which arise from the carrying on of the regulated activity,

(c) maintain securely an accurate, complete and contemporaneous record in respect of each service user, including a record of the care and treatment provided to the service user and of decisions taken in relation to the care and treatment provided;

(d) maintain securely such other records as are necessary to be kept in relation to—

(i) persons employed in the carrying on of the regulated activity, and

©Crown Copyright

Appendix 1

(ii) the management of the regulated activity;

(e) seek and act on feedback from relevant persons and other persons on the services provided in the carrying on of the regulated activity, for the purposes of continually evaluating and improving such services;

(f) evaluate and improve their practice in respect of the processing of the information referred to in sub-paragraphs (a) to (e).

(3) The registered person must send to the Commission, when requested to do so and by no later than 28 days beginning on the day after receipt of the request—

(a) a written report setting out how, and the extent to which, in the opinion of the registered person, the requirements of paragraph (2)(a) and

(b) are being complied with, and (b) any plans that the registered person has for improving the standard of the services provided to service users with a view to ensuring their health and welfare.

18. Staffing

(1) Sufficient numbers of suitably qualified, competent, skilled and experienced persons must be deployed in order to meet the requirements of this Part.

(2) Persons employed by the service provider in the provision of a regulated activity must—

(a) receive such appropriate support, training, professional development, supervision and appraisal as is necessary to enable them to carry out the duties they are employed to perform,

(b) be enabled where appropriate to obtain further qualifications appropriate to the work they perform, and

(c) where such persons are health care professionals, social workers or other professionals registered with a health care or social care regulator, be enabled to provide evidence to the regulator in question

©Crown Copyright

Appendix 1

demonstrating, where it is possible to do so, that they continue to meet the professional standards which are a condition of their ability to practise or a requirement of their role.

19. Fit and proper persons employed

(1) Persons employed for the purposes of carrying on a regulated activity must—

    (a) be of good character,

    (b) have the qualifications, competence, skills and experience which are necessary for the work to be performed by them, and

    (c) be able by reason of their health, after reasonable adjustments are made, of properly performing tasks which are intrinsic to the work for which they are employed.

(2) Recruitment procedures must be established and operated effectively to ensure that persons employed meet the conditions in—

    (a) paragraph (1), or

    (b) in a case to which regulation 5 applies, paragraph (3) of that regulation.

(3) The following information must be available in relation to each such person employed—

    (a) the information specified in Schedule 3, and

    (b) such other information as is required under any enactment to be kept by the registered person in relation to such persons employed.

(4) Persons employed must be registered with the relevant professional body where such registration is required by, or under, any enactment in relation to—

    (a) the work that the person is to perform, or

    (b) the title that the person takes or uses.

©Crown Copyright

Appendix 1

(5) Where a person employed by the registered person no longer meets the criteria in paragraph (1), the registered person must—

(a) take such action as is necessary and proportionate to ensure that the requirement in that paragraph is complied with, and

(b) if the person is a health care professional, social worker or other professional registered with a health care or social care regulator, inform the regulator in question.

(6) Paragraphs (1) and (3) of this regulation do not apply in a case to which regulation 5 applies.

20. Duty of candour

(1) A health service body must act in an open and transparent way with relevant persons in relation to care and treatment provided to service users in carrying on a regulated activity.

(2) As soon as reasonably practicable after becoming aware that a notifiable safety incident has occurred a health service body must—

(a) notify the relevant person that the incident has occurred in accordance with paragraph (3), and

(b) provide reasonable support to the relevant person in relation to the incident, including when giving such notification.

(3) The notification to be given under paragraph (2)(a) must—

(a) be given in person by one or more representatives of the health service body,

(b) provide an account, which to the best of the health service body's knowledge is true, of all the facts the health service body knows about the incident as at the date of the notification,

(c) advise the relevant person what further enquiries into the incident the health service body believes are appropriate,

(d) include an apology, and

©Crown Copyright

Appendix 1

(e) be recorded in a written record which is kept securely by the health service body.

(4) The notification given under paragraph (2)(a) must be followed by a written notification given or sent to the relevant person containing—

(a) the information provided under paragraph (3)(b),

(b) details of any enquiries to be undertaken in accordance with paragraph (3)(c),

(c) the results of any further enquiries into the incident, and

(d) an apology.

(5) But if the relevant person cannot be contacted in person or declines to speak to the representative of the health service body—

(a) paragraphs (2) to (4) are not to apply, and

(b) a written record is to be kept of attempts to contact or to speak to the relevant person.

(6) The health service body must keep a copy of all correspondence with the relevant person under paragraph (4).

(7) In this regulation— "apology" means an expression of sorrow or regret in respect of a notifiable safety incident; "moderate harm" means—

(a) harm that requires a moderate increase in treatment, and

(b) significant, but not permanent, harm; "moderate increase in treatment" means an unplanned return to surgery, an unplanned readmission, a prolonged episode of care, extra time in hospital or as an outpatient, cancelling of treatment, or transfer to another treatment area (such as intensive care); "notifiable safety incident" means any unintended or unexpected incident that occurred in respect of a service user during the provision of a regulated activity that, in the reasonable opinion of a health care professional, could result in, or appears to have resulted in—

(a) the death of the service user, where the death relates directly to the incident rather than to the natural course of the service user's illness or underlying condition, or

©Crown Copyright

Appendix 1

(b) severe harm, moderate harm or prolonged psychological harm to the service user; "prolonged psychological harm" means psychological harm which a service user has experienced, or is likely to experience, for a continuous period of at least 28 days; "relevant person" means the service user or, in the following circumstances, a person lawfully acting on their behalf—

(a) on the death of the service user,

(b) where the service user is under 16 and not competent to make a decision in relation to their care or treatment, or

(c) where the service user is 16 or over and lacks capacity (as determined in accordance with sections 2 and 3 of the 2005 Act) in relation to the matter;

"severe harm" means a permanent lessening of bodily, sensory, motor, physiologic or intellectual functions, including removal of the wrong limb or organ or brain damage, that is related directly to the incident and not related to the natural course of the service user's illness or underlying condition.

[...]

End of Appendix 1

Appendix 2: Code of Conduct

Reproduced under permission from Skills for Care, © Skills for Care & Skills for Health 2013. This document can be found in its original form at www.skillsforcare.org.uk & www.skillsforhealth.org.uk

Last updated: 22 November 2018

Code of Conduct for Healthcare Support Workers and Adult Social Care Workers in England

As a Healthcare Support Worker or an Adult Social Care Worker, you make a valuable and important contribution to the delivery of high quality healthcare, **care and support**.

Following the guidance set out in this Code of Conduct will give you the reassurance that you are providing safe and **compassionate** care of a high standard, and the confidence to challenge others who are not. This Code will also tell the public and people who use health and care services exactly what they should expect from Healthcare Support Workers and Adult Social Care Workers in England.

As a Healthcare Support Worker or Adult Social Care Worker in England you must:

1. Be **accountable** by making sure you can answer for your actions or **omissions**.

2. **Promote** and **uphold** the privacy, **dignity**, **rights**, health and **wellbeing** of people who use health and care services and their carers at all times.

3. Work in **collaboration** with your colleagues to ensure the delivery of high quality, safe and compassionate healthcare, care and support.

4. Communicate in an open, and **effective** way to promote the health, safety and wellbeing of people who use health and care services and their carers.

5. Respect a person's right to confidentiality.

Appendix 2

6. Strive to improve the quality of healthcare, care and support through **continuing professional development**.

7. Uphold and promote equality, **diversity** and inclusion.

Purpose

This Code is based on the principles of protecting the public by promoting best practice. It will ensure that you are 'working to standard', providing high quality, **compassionate** healthcare, **care and support**.

The Code describes the standards of conduct, behaviour and attitude that the public and people who use health and care services should expect. You are responsible for, and have a duty of care to ensure that your conduct does not fall below the standards detailed in the Code. Nothing that you do, or **omit** to do, should harm the safety and **wellbeing** of people who use health and care services, and the public.

Scope

These standards apply to you if you are a:

- **Healthcare Support Worker** (including an Assistant Practitioner) in England who reports to a Registered Nurse or Midwife. Healthcare Support Workers reporting to other healthcare professionals are not currently included.

- **Adult Social Care Worker** in England. This could either be in an independent capacity (for example, as a Personal Assistant); for a residential care provider; or as a supported living, day support or domiciliary care worker. The Code does not apply to Social Work Assistants.

How does the Code help me as a Healthcare Support Worker or an Adult Social Care Worker?

It provides a set of clear standards, so you:

- can be sure of the standards you are expected to meet.

Appendix 2

- can know whether you are working to these standards, or if you need to change the way you are working.
- can identify areas for continuing professional development.
- can fulfil the requirements of your role, behave correctly and do the right thing at all times. This is essential to protect people who use health and care services, the public and others from harm.

How does this Code help people who use health and care services and members of the public?

The Code helps the public and those who use health and care services to understand what standards they can expect of Healthcare Support Workers and Adult Social Care Workers. The Code aims to give people who use health and care services the confidence that they will be treated with **dignity**, **respect** and **compassion** at all times.

How does this Code help my employer?

The Code helps employers to understand what standards they should expect of Healthcare Support Workers and Adult Social Care Workers. If there are people who do not meet these standards, it will help to identify them and their support and training needs.

Glossary

You can find a glossary of terms and key words (shown in **bold** throughout the Code) at the end of the document.

The Code

1. Be accountable by making sure you can answer for your actions or omissions

Guidance statements

Appendix 2

As a Healthcare Support Worker or Adult Social Care Worker in England, you must:

1. be honest with yourself and others about what you can do, recognise your abilities and the limitations of your **competence** and only carry out or delegate those tasks agreed in your job description and for which you are **competent**.

2. always behave and present yourself in a way that does not call into question your suitability to work in a health and social care environment.

3. be able to justify and be **accountable** for your actions or your **omissions** – what you fail to do.

4. always ask your supervisor or employer for guidance if you do not feel able or adequately prepared to carry out any aspect of your work, or if you are unsure how to **effectively** deliver a task.

5. tell your supervisor or employer about any issues that might affect your ability to do your job **competently** and safely. If you do not feel **competent** to carry out an activity, you must report this.

6. establish and maintain clear and appropriate professional boundaries in your relationships with people who use health and care services, carers and colleagues at all times.

7. never accept any offers of loans, gifts, benefits or hospitality from anyone you are supporting or anyone close to them which may be seen to compromise your position.

8. comply with your employers' **agreed ways of working**.

9. report any actions or **omissions** by yourself or colleagues that you feel may compromise the safety or care of people who use health and care services and, if necessary use **whistleblowing** procedures to report any suspected wrongdoing.

2. Promote and uphold the privacy, dignity, rights, health and wellbeing of people who use health and care services and their carers at all times

Appendix 2

Guidance statements

As a Healthcare Support Worker or Adult Social Care Worker in England you must:

1. always act in the **best interests** of people who use health and care services.

2. always treat people with **respect** and **compassion**.

3. put the needs, goals and aspirations of people who use health and care services first, helping them to be in control and to choose the healthcare, **care and support** they receive.

4. **promote** people's independence and ability to **self-care**, assisting those who use health and care services to exercise their rights and make informed choices.

5. always gain **valid consent** before providing healthcare, **care and support**. You must also **respect** a person's right to refuse to receive healthcare, **care and support** if they are capable of doing so.

6. always maintain the privacy and **dignity** of people who use health and care services, their carers and others.

7. be alert to any changes that could affect a person's needs or progress and report your observations in line with your employer's **agreed ways of working**.

8. always make sure that your actions or **omissions** do not harm an individual's health or **wellbeing**. You must never **abuse**, neglect, **harm** or exploit those who use health and care services, their carers or your colleagues.

9. challenge and report dangerous, abusive, discriminatory or exploitative behaviour or practice.

10. always take comments and complaints seriously, respond to them in line with **agreed ways of working** and inform a senior member of staff.

Appendix 2

3. Work in collaboration with your colleagues to ensure the delivery of high quality, safe and compassionate healthcare, care and support

Guidance statements

> As a Healthcare Support Worker or Adult Social Care Worker in England you must:
>
> 1. understand and value your contribution and the vital part you play in your team.
>
> 2. recognise and **respect** the roles and expertise of your colleagues both in the team and from other agencies and disciplines, and work in partnership with them.
>
> 3. work openly and co-operatively with colleagues including those from other disciplines and agencies, and treat them with **respect**.
>
> 4. work openly and co-operatively with people who use health and care services and their families or carers and treat them with **respect**.
>
> 5. honour your work commitments, agreements and arrangements and be reliable, dependable and trustworthy.
>
> 6. actively encourage the delivery of high quality healthcare, **care and support**.

4. Communicate in an open and effective way to promote the health, safety and wellbeing of people who use health and care services and their carers

Guidance statements

> As a Healthcare Support Worker or Adult Social Care Worker in England you must:
>
> 1. communicate **respectfully** with people who use health and care services and their carers in an open, accurate, effective, straightforward and confidential way.

Appendix 2

2. communicate **effectively** and consult with your colleagues as appropriate.

3. always explain and discuss the care, support or procedure you intend to carry out with the person and only continue if they give **valid consent**.

4. maintain clear and accurate records of the healthcare, **care and support** you provide. Immediately report to a senior member of staff any changes or concerns you have about a person's condition.

5. recognise both the extent and the limits of your role, knowledge and **competence** when communicating with people who use health and care services, carers and colleagues.

5. Respect people's right to confidentiality

Guidance statements

As a Healthcare Support Worker or Adult Social Care Worker in England you must:

1. treat all information about people who use health and care services and their carers as confidential.

2. only discuss or **disclose** information about people who use health and care services and their carers in accordance with legislation and **agreed ways of working**.

3. always seek guidance from a senior member of staff regarding any information or issues that you are concerned about.

4. always discuss issues of disclosure with a senior member of staff.

6. Strive to improve the quality of healthcare, care and support through continuing professional development

Guidance statements

As a Healthcare Support Worker or Adult Social Care Worker in England you must:

Appendix 2

1. ensure up to date compliance with all statutory and mandatory training, in agreement with your supervisor.

2. participate in **continuing professional development** to achieve the **competence** required for your role.

3. carry out **competence-based** training and education in line with your **agreed ways of working.**

4. improve the quality and safety of the care you provide with the help of your supervisor (and a mentor if available), and in line with your **agreed ways of working**.

5. maintain an up-to-date record of your training and development.

6. contribute to the learning and development of others as appropriate.

7. Uphold and promote equality, diversity and inclusion

Guidance statements

As a Healthcare Support Worker or Adult Social Care Worker in England you must:

1. **respect** the **individuality** and **diversity** of the people who use health and care services, their carers and your colleagues.

2. not **discriminate** or condone discrimination against people who use health and care services, their carers or your colleagues.

3. **promote** equal opportunities and inclusion for the people who use health and care services and their carers.

4. report any concerns regarding **equality**, **diversity** and **inclusion** to a senior member of staff as soon as possible.

Glossary of terms

ACCOUNTABLE: accountability is to be responsible for the decisions you make and answerable for your actions.

Appendix 2

AGREED WAYS OF WORKING: includes policies and procedures where these exist; they may be less formally documented among individual employers and the self-employed.

BEST INTERESTS: the Mental Capacity Act (2005) sets out a checklist of things to consider when deciding what's in a person's 'best interests'.

CARE AND SUPPORT: care and support enables people to do the everyday things like getting out of bed, dressed and into work; cooking meals; seeing friends; caring for our families; and being part of our communities. It might include emotional support at a time of difficulty or stress, or helping people who are caring for a family member or friend. It can mean support from community groups or networks: for example, giving others a lift to a social event. It might also include state-funded support, such as information and advice, support for carers, housing support, disability benefits and adult social care.

COLLABORATION: the action of working with someone to achieve a common goal.

COMPASSION: descriptions of compassionate care include:, dignity and comfort: taking time and patience to listen, explain and communicate; demonstrating empathy, kindness and warmth; care centred around an individual person's needs, involving people in the decisions about their healthcare, care and support.

COMPETENCE: the knowledge, skills, attitudes and ability to practise safely and effectively without the need for direct supervision.

COMPETENT: having the necessary ability, knowledge, or skill to do something successfully.

CONTINUING PROFESSIONAL DEVELOPMENT: this is the way in which a worker continues to learn and develop throughout their careers, keeping their skills and knowledge up to date and ensuring they can work safely and effectively.

DIGNITY: covers all aspects of daily life, including respect, privacy, autonomy and self-worth. While dignity may be difficult to define, what is clear is that people know when they have not been treated with dignity and respect. Dignity is about interpersonal behaviours as well as systems and processes.

Appendix 2

DISCRIMINATE: discrimination can be the result of prejudice, misconception and stereotyping. Whether this behaviour is intentional or unintentional does not excuse it. It is the perception of the person discriminated against that is important.

DIVERSITY: celebrating differences and valuing everyone. Diversity encompasses visible and non-visible individual differences and is about respecting those differences.

EFFECTIVE: to be successful in producing a desired or intended result.

EQUALITY: being equal in status, rights, and opportunities.

INCLUSION: ensuring that people are treated equally and fairly and are included as part of society.

MENTOR: mentoring is a work-based method of training using existing experienced staff to transfer their skills informally or semi-formally to learners.

OMISSION: to leave out or exclude.

PROMOTE: to support or actively encourage.

RESPECT: to have due regard for someone's feelings, wishes, or rights.12

SELF-CARE: this refers to the practices undertaken by people towards maintaining health and wellbeing and managing their own care needs. It has been defined as: "the actions people take for themselves, their children and their families to stay fit and maintain good physical and mental health; meet social and psychological needs; prevent illness or accidents; care for minor ailments and long-term conditions; and maintain health and wellbeing after an acute illness or discharge from hospital." (Self care – A real choice: Self care support – A practical option, published by Department of Health, 2005).

UPHOLD: to maintain a custom or practice.

VALID CONSENT: for consent to be valid, it must be given voluntarily by an appropriately informed person who has the capacity to consent to the intervention in question. This will be the patient, the person who uses health and care services or someone with parental responsibility for a person under the age of 18, someone authorised to do so under a Lasting Power of Attorney (LPA) or someone who has the authority to make treatment

Appendix 2

decisions as a court appointed deputy). Agreement where the person does not know what the intervention entails is not 'consent'.

WELLBEING: a person's wellbeing may include their sense of hope, confidence, self-esteem, ability to communicate their wants and needs, ability to make contact with other people, ability to show warmth and affection, experience and showing of pleasure or enjoyment.

WHISTLEBLOWING: whistleblowing is when a worker reports suspected wrongdoing at work. Officially this is called 'making a disclosure in the public interest' and may sometimes be referred to as 'escalating concerns.' You must report things that you feel are not right, are illegal or if anyone at work is neglecting their duties. This includes when someone's health and safety is in danger; damage to the environment; a criminal offence; that the company is not obeying the law (like not having the right insurance); or covering up wrongdoing.

End of Appendix 2

Author's bibliography to 2019 in chronological order

Note: ASIN stands for *Amazon Standard Identification Number* and you can use it in order to locate my books in your local Amazon marketplace, for example *Amazon.com*, or *Amazon.co.uk*, or *Amazon.es*.

-Matthews, Alex (2017) *Rebirth: Unconscious Mind Programming. A step-by-step guide to becoming wiser, freer and younger.* Kindle Direct Publishing. ASIN: B075T7J3PS Paperback available Amazon 2017. ASIN: 1549819704
https://www.amazon.co.uk/dp/B075T7J3PS

-Matthews, Alex (2016) *She'll be Alright: a story-based approach to exploring issues of hidden neglect in care homes. A training and self-study guide with a focus on dementia care.* Pavilion Publishing and Media Ltd. UK.
https://www.pavpub.com/shell-be-alright/

-Matthews, Alex (2016) *The Adventures of Quito the Mosquito.* English edition. Kindle Direct Publishing. ASIN: B01LYFDYX3
https://www.amazon.co.uk/dp/B01LYFDYX3

-Matthews, Alex (2016) *Quito's Birthday.* English/Spanish edition. Kindle Direct Publishing. ASIN: B01JKOPRQS
https://www.amazon.co.uk/dp/B01JKOPRQS

-Matthews, Alex (2016) *Quito and Khaki the Frog.* English/Spanish edition. Kindle Direct Publishing. ASIN: B01F9AGFB8
https://www.amazon.co.uk/dp/B01F9AGFB8

-Matthews, Alex (2016) *Quito the Mosquito.* English/Spanish edition. Kindle Direct Publishing. ASIN: B01EZ24Y46
https://www.amazon.co.uk/dp/B01EZ24Y46

About the autor

Alex Matthews has worked as a teacher, translator and care researcher since 1990. Having read Linguistics at Southampton University, his first specialism is teaching English as a Foreign Language, but Alex is currently (as of 2019) doing research into alternatives to the current elderly care model in the UK. Alex has published a care guide, a novel, and several children's stories.

Contact
Alex Matthews can be contacted through his blog:
http://isladeoro.blogspot.co.uk

Printed in Great Britain
by Amazon